# The Bean Queen's Cookbook

*May you eat well
and be well.
Karen R. Hurd*

## By
## Karen R. Hurd, Nutritionist
## and
## Jeanne Hutchinson

**Acknowledgements**

Photography:  Abigail Hamm

Typing and layout:  Sandy Edwards, Becky Voetmann, Joshua Hurd, Kathryn Bartelt

Test kitchen chef:  Kathryn Bartelt

Test kitchen help:  Ruth Voetmann, Ellie Bergbrader

**Other publications by Karen R. Hurd**

> *And They Said It Wasn't Possible*
> Book, 2006

> *If You Eat Like the Devil, You'll Feel Like the Devil*
> DVD/CD, 2008

> *A Five-Pronged Approach to Weight Loss*
> DVD/CD, 2008

> *Depression and Anxiety*
> DVD/CD, 2009

> *Inflammatory Disorders—Arthritis and Fibromyalgia*
> DVD/CD, 2009

> *The Fountain of Youth: How to Slow the Process of Aging*
> DVD/CD, 2011

> *Children's Health, from Infancy to Adulthood*
> DVD/CD, 2012

> *Myths that Muddle: Nutritious or Not?*
> DVD/CD, 2013

> *Cancer: A Nutritional Intervention*
> DVD/CD, 2013

> *Allergies*
> DVD/CD, 2014

*To my clients*

*who encouraged me to publish a bean cookbook*

Order this book online at www.KarenHurd.com or by calling 715-877-3510.

Printed in Eau Claire, Wisconsin by ECPrinting.

ISBN: 978-0-9916158-0-3

Scene and Hurd Publications
phone: 715-877-3510   fax: 715-877-2699
www.KarenHurd.com

# Table of Contents

# Preface

Since 1994 when I opened my nutritional practice, I have known that I would need to publish a cookbook at some point. As the consumption of legumes is a critical part of most every person's plan for healing, the need for a bean cookbook became evident. There are other bean cookbooks that have been published; however, the use of sugar, molasses, honey, or other sweeteners are prolific in those recipes. These are additions that I cannot endorse because they do not add but rather subtract from a person's health.

At the request of my clients and in light of the need for a cookbook that gave innovative recipes that were unquestionably healthy, I began the process of creating a cookbook. My first and foremost problem was that I was not the person to create the recipes. My nutritional practice is a busy one; I had neither the time nor the creative talent to devise the needed recipes. Through a providential meeting I came in contact with a woman who had the needed skills and desire, and who would be able to accomplish the task I set before her.

That task was a daunting one. I asked her to create three hundred bean recipes in one year. I gave her specific guidance on what could be used as ingredients and what could not be used. Jeanne Hutchinson began the work. She used her imagination and inventive skills to devise the recipes. She tested and retested each recipe in her kitchen until she felt that it was exactly right. Then the recipe was sent to my kitchen where my twenty-five year old daughter, Kathryn, took on the job of being the test kitchen cook. Every Friday was Bean Cookbook Day. Jeanne's recipes were made, tasted by me, my family, and my nutritional practice staff.

There was yet another important component to consider. Had anyone seen a bean biscuit before? Who would know the appearance of a finished bean loaf? What would bean mashed "potatoes" look like? I needed a professional photographer. Abigail Hamm was just the person. She arrived in the kitchen on the Bean Cookbook Days and spent hours artfully arranging and photographing the recipes to appeal to the appetite.

Some may wonder at the title of the book, *The Bean Queen's Cookbook*. For years my clients have called me the Bean Queen because of the consistent and persistent advice that I continue to loudly emphasize—eat beans! The name "Bean Queen" became even more attached to my identity when I was dubbed the Bean Queen by Mark Halvorsen on his radio program Front Page (WWIB 103.7 FM, Eau Claire/Chippewa Falls, Wisconsin). I am privileged to be a guest on this show twice a month.

I must recognize all my clients that submitted bean recipes. Jeanne examined, tested, and tweaked them; although some were great just as submitted. However, I must credit Jeanne with the creation of the vast majority of the recipes in this book. She took the directives that I gave her and created these wonderful dishes.

I am appreciative of all the skill and talent that Jeanne Hutchinson has brought in these recipes. She and I are pleased to present you with an excellent cookbook that will be a resource of good health to you and your family.

Karen R. Hurd, Nutritionist
Karen R. Hurd Nutritional Practice, LLC
P.O. Box 159
114 South State Street
Fall Creek, Wisconsin   54742
715-877-3510
www.karenhurd.com

# About Beans

## By Karen R. Hurd, Nutritionist

Sorely neglected in the United States, yet in most other countries a daily staple of life, beans are one of the best foods on the planet Earth. They provide a rich source of complex carbohydrates, minerals, saponins, polyphenolics, and some amino acids; but towering above all of these necessary nutrients is the hallmark and crowning glory of the bean—soluble fiber.

Soluble fiber is a remarkable substance. It has the capacity to bind with fats and prevent their absorption. This is certainly of interest when eating things such as bacon or fried foods where the blocking of those not-so-healthy fats is desired. However, the binding capacity of soluble fiber to the digestive fluid bile is the greatest work that soluble fiber accomplishes.

Bile is a vehicle that the liver uses to discard fat-soluble waste. The liver clears all fat-soluble waste from the bloodstream and places it into bile. Bile is made from fat, specifically, triglycerides. Fat-soluble wastes are substances that create problems for the human body if left to circulate the blood stream. Therefore, the riddance of them is an essential part of health.

However, because bile is made from fat, it will be absorbed in the human intestine—in fact 90-95% is absorbed! Therefore, all the waste products that were carried in the bile are also re-deposited into the blood stream. Soluble fiber provides a solution to this problem. It binds to the bile and prevents its absorption. Soluble fiber cannot cross the intestinal barrier, and whatever is bound to it cannot cross the intestinal barrier. By discarding the toxin-laden bile, we prevent many health problems.

For the best of health, I recommend the consumption of fifteen grams of soluble fiber per day. It is important to note that the frequency of consumption is the critical issue. Doubling up on servings will not provide the benefit desired. Each person should consume five grams of soluble fiber at breakfast, five grams at the noon meal, and five grams at the evening meal. The soluble fiber binds with the bile that is present in the duodenum (the first part of the small intestine) at the time of consumption. Later, more bile will be delivered to the duodenum; therefore, another serving of soluble fiber is needed.

I need to address the actual content of soluble fiber in a bean. First, know that many factors affect the soluble fiber content of a bean. How long the bean remains on the vine before it is harvested, the amount of sun and rain the bean received, the soil quality, species of plant, and the processing of the bean after harvesting. Additionally, cooking actually increases the content of soluble fiber. Having consulted several sources, I have determined an average amount of soluble fiber that I will use as a standard in this cookbook. The importance in having an average number of grams of soluble fiber is that people need to know how many beans they must eat to obtain the recommended five grams of soluble fiber per meal. As the variables that affect the soluble fiber content are many and some uncontrollable (i.e. weather), I have averaged the numbers from the sources that I consulted, and then taken into consideration the cooking time (which increases the amount of soluble fiber).

The working number that I have used in this cookbook is ¼ cup of bean flour (that has been cooked in a recipe—regardless of the type of bean flour) contains approximately five grams of soluble fiber. One-half cup of cooked beans contains approximately five grams of soluble fiber. Again, please note that this is only an estimated amount as the true amount of soluble fiber varies widely from bean to bean and is dependent on a multitude of factors.

Sources consulted:
"Dietary Fiber Content and Composition of Vegetables Determined by Two Methods of Analysis," *Journal of Agricultural and Food Chemistry*, 41, 1608-1612, American Chemical Society, 1993.

"Dietary fiber content of commonly fresh and cooked vegetables consumed in India," Khanum, Swamy, Krishna, Santhanam, Viswanathan, *Biochemistry and Nutrition Discipline*, Kluver Academic Publishers, Netherlands, Feb 2000.

"Dietary fiber content of selected foods," Anderson, Bridges, *American Journal of Clinical Nutrition*, 47:440-7, 1988.

"Effect of Fermentation and Autoclaving on Dietary Fiber Fractions and Antinutritional Factors of Beans (Phaseolus vulgaris L.)," Martin-Cabrejas, Sanfiz, Vidal, Molla, Esteban, Lopez-Andreu, *Journal of Agriculture and Food Chemistry*, Volume 52, Number 2, American Chemical Society, Jan 2004.

"Investigation of Factors That Affect the Solubility of Dietary Fiber, as Nonstarch Polysaccharides, in Seed Tissues of Mung Bean (Vigna radiate) and Black Gram (Vigna mungo)," Gooneratne, Majsak-Newman, Robertson, and Selvendran, *Journal of Agricultural and Food Chemistry*, Volume 42, Number 3, American Chemical Society, March 1994.

*Krause's Food Nutrition and Diet Therapy*, Mahan, Escott-Stump, Philadelphia, WB Saunders Co, 1996.

Northwestern University—Feinberg School of Medicine—listing of soluble fiber content of foods.

*The CRC Handbook of Dietary Fiber in Human Nutrition*, 3rd ed., Spiller, London, CRC Press, 2001.

Tufts University Nutrition Unit—listing of soluble fiber content of foods.

United States Department of Agriculture—listing of soluble fiber content of foods.

# Getting Started

## A Word About Brands

We have tried to be as generic as possible as far as brand-name products in the recording of the recipes included in *The Bean Queen's Cookbook*. In this way, the recipes can reach beyond regional and even national borders. However, some may find it useful to know the following:

Better than Bouillon™ is the bouillon paste that we used in all our recipes.

Tabasco® sauce is the red pepper sauce that was used.

Bragg's® Liquid Aminos is the soy liquid aminos that was used.

Hebrew National® beef franks were used in the few recipes that called for franks.

Tony Chachere's® Creole seasoning is the referenced Creole seasoning.

Good Seasons® Sun Dried Tomato Vinaigrette with Roasted Red Peppers is the brand of sun-dried tomato vinaigrette that was used.

In recipes where mayonaisse is called for, a salad dressing/sandwich spread will not yield as good a result. All recipes that call for mayonaisse in this book refer to real mayonaisse.

Turkey bacon was used in the recipes (where called for); however, any bacon can be substituted for the turkey bacon. Turkey bacon usually needs to be fried in a little oil to cause it to crisp and brown, whereas other bacon (pork) will need no additional oil when frying.

Almond milk is an ingredient that is frequently called for in these recipes. Almond milk can be easily made (see page 107), or a purchased almond milk can be used. Be sure to buy unsweetened and plain, not vanilla.

## Kitchen Equipment

There are a few things that will make using this cookbook easier:

<u>Utensils:</u>  measuring cups and spoons, spatulas, heat-resistant slotted spoon, wooden spoon, whisk, vegetable peeler, small trigger-style scoop, a chef's knife, plastic lettuce knife, cutting boards or silicone cutting pads, and a timer.

<u>Mixing bowls:</u> various sizes.  Lettuce will brown in metal bowls.  Glass or plastic bowls work best.

<u>Colander:</u>  when straining lentils or any of the smaller beans and peas be sure to use a colander with small holes.

<u>Blender:</u>  for grinding and pureeing.

<u>Food Processor:</u>  probably the most utilized piece of equipment in these recipes!  It will chop, grind, and puree, making a cook's work much simpler.

<u>Slow cooker:</u>  use the right size for the recipe.  If crock is too large, food will cook too quickly and dry out.  If a large slow cooker is the only one available, double the recipe to fill the crock properly.  Do not fill more than ¾ full.  Avoid lid-lifting as it lets the heat out and extra cooking time may be needed.

<u>Non-stick skillets:</u>  various sizes.

<u>Sauce pans:</u>  various sizes.

<u>Dutch oven or soup pot:</u>  a Dutch oven is a heavy iron pot with a tightly-fitting lid; however, any large soup pot with a lid will work.

<u>Casserole dishes:</u>  various sizes.

<u>Loaf pans:</u>  various sizes.

<u>Baking sheets:</u>  also commonly known as cookie sheets.

<u>Disposables:</u>  parchment paper, foil, plastic wrap, zipper-style storage bags, and cheese cloth.

## Just a few of the bean
## varieties available for your cooking pleasure.

Top, left to right:
Dried red lentils, dried lentils,  dried yellow split peas,
dried green split peas,  dried baby lima beans, black beans.
Middle, left to right:
Butter beans, red beans, Great Northern beans, lima beans,
cannellini beans, pinto beans.
Bottom, left to right:
Garbanzo beans  (chickpeas), red kidney beans, navy beans, black-eyed peas.

## Cooking Dried Beans

**1 cup dried beans**
**3-4 cups water for soaking**
**Water for cooking**

### Sort and Rinse Beans:
Pour beans into a large bowl or onto a baking sheet. Carefully sort through beans, removing any stones, debris, or damaged beans. Pour beans into a colander, rinse well, and drain.

### Traditional Soaking Method:
Place beans and water for soaking into a large bowl. Let soak in a cool place at least 4 hours (overnight is best). Rinse, drain, and cook.

### Quick Soaking Method:
Place beans into a large pot and add soaking water. Bring to a boil. Reduce heat to medium and cook for 2-3 minutes. Remove from heat, cover, and let stand at least 1 hour. Drain beans and rinse in a colander. Cook according to recipe or cover and refrigerate for up to 3 days if not using the beans immediately.

### Extra-Quick Soaking Method:
Place beans into a large pot and add soaking water. Bring to a boil. Reduce heat to medium and continue boiling for 10 minutes. Drain beans in a colander. Place beans back in pot and add 3-4 cups (or more) fresh water. Water should be 2" above beans. Let soak 30 minutes. Rinse, drain, and cook.

### Cooking:
Place soaked beans into a large pot. Cover beans with fresh cold water, about 3" above beans. Bring to a boil. Reduce heat and simmer gently. Do not let boil while simmering or skins will burst open. Taste-test for tenderness. Try several from the center of the pot. Beans should be tender but not mushy. Do not over-cook.

### Cooking Time Chart:

| Soaked Beans | Cooking Time |
| --- | --- |
| Black Beans | 30-35 minutes |
| Small Red Beans | 30-35 minutes |
| Pinto Beans | 30-35 minutes |
| Navy Beans | 35-40 minutes |
| Red or White Kidney Beans | 35-40 minutes |
| Great Northern Beans | 40-45 minutes |
| Lima Beans | 55-60 minutes |
| Garbanzo Beans/Chickpeas | 80 minutes |

## Pressure Cooking:

Beans can be cooked in a pressure cooker in as little as 15-20 minutes. Use the manufacturer's directions. Do not overfill pressure cooker, and cook with no more than 10-15 pounds of pressure. To prevent foam from coming up through the pressure valve, add 1 Tbsp. vegetable oil to the beans.

## Substituting Home-Cooked Beans for Canned Beans:

If you prefer to make your own beans, a 14-16-oz. can equals about 1½ cups of cooked beans. A 19-oz. can is about 2¼ cups of cooked beans. Cooked beans can be frozen in freezer containers or zipper-style storage bags, thawed, and used in place of canned beans in any recipe. Be sure to label and date containers. Beans can be stored in freezer for up to 3 months.

## Dried Beans in a Crockpot

**1 lb. or 2 cups dried beans, sorted & rinsed**
**Water**
**2 tsp. salt**

Pour beans into a 3 or 4 quart slow cooker. Fill slow cooker with water to 1 inch from top. Do not use salt or turn slow cooker on. Let soak 8-10 hours or overnight. Drain beans in colander and place back in slow cooker. Cover with fresh water to 1 inch from top. Add salt to water. Cook on low for 10 hours. Drain and refrigerate or freeze. Makes about 6 cups of cooked beans.

This hassle-free method of preparing beans will work for most dry beans: adzuki beans, black or turtle beans, chickpeas or garbanzo beans, lima beans, navy beans, Great Northern beans, cannellini or white kidney beans, red kidney beans, small red or Mexican beans, and pinto beans. Cooking times will vary with the size of crockpot used.

## Cooking Dried Split Peas

**1 lb. or 2 cups dried green or yellow split peas**
**8 cups hot water**

**No-Soaking Method:** Split peas require no soaking. Sort and rinse peas. Place split peas and water into a large pot. Cover and bring to a boil. Reduce heat and simmer (slow boil under surface of water) for 20-25 minutes (just until tender) for salads; 30 minutes for purees, vegetables and main dishes; and 45 minutes for soups.

**Soaking Method:** Sort and rinse peas. Using 2-3 times as much water as peas, allow peas to soak for 8 hours. Drain and rinse. Place split peas in a large pot and cover with water. Bring water to a boil, reduce heat, and simmer for 15 minutes. Taste for tenderness. Drain.

## Cooking Dried Black-Eyed Peas

**1 lb. or 2 cups dried black-eyed peas**
**6 cups water**

Sort and rinse black-eyed peas. Black-eyed peas require no soaking. Place peas and water into a large pot. Bring water to a boil. Reduce heat. Cover and simmer (slow boil under the surface of water) for 30-40 minutes, until tender but not mushy. Drain.

## Cooking Dried Lentils

**1 lb. or 2⅔ cups dried lentils**
**8 cups hot water**

Sort and rinse lentils. Lentils require no soaking. Place lentils and water into a large pot. Bring water to a boil. Reduce heat. Simmer uncovered for 15-20 minutes, stirring occasionally. Test for tenderness after 15 minutes. Continue simmering another 5 minutes, if necessary. Drain. One pound of dried lentils will yield 6-6½ cups of cooked lentils. Lentils will firm up when chilled.

## Tips

Dried beans should be stored in airtight containers and not in the plastic bags in which they are purchased. Dried beans will keep for up to 6 months in the cupboard.

If beans are not tender in the allotted cooking time, they are either too old; the altitude is high (need to cook longer); or hard water is used (need to cook longer). If using hard water, add ¼ tsp. baking soda for every 2 cups dried beans when cooking.

Beans, lentils, and split peas all freeze well. Store in zipper-style freezer bags. Beans can be frozen in 1½ cup portions and substituted for any 14-16-oz. can of beans in any recipe. Lentils and split-peas can be frozen in 1 cup portions for use in recipes.

Be sure to always cook at the temperature noted in each recipe. If the recipe says simmer, then simmer; do not boil. If it says boil, do not simmer, etc. This makes a measurable difference in the texture of the beans, lentils, and split peas which can turn out too hard or too mushy.

Cooked beans can be stored up to 4 days in the refrigerator and up to 3 months in the freezer. Label and date freezer bags. Individual portions of beans can be frozen in small zipper-style freezer bags and stored together in a larger bag that is labeled and dated.

Beans are interchangeable in any recipe. Substitute your favorite beans for the beans listed.

# Appetizers & Snacks

## Black Bean and Avocado Salsa

1 15-oz. can black beans, rinsed
   & drained
3 Roma tomatoes, diced
½ small red or sweet onion, diced
½ avocado, diced
2 small cloves garlic, minced
1 Tbsp. chopped fresh parsley
3 Tbsp. lime juice, divided

Combine all ingredients except 1 Tbsp. lime juice. Stir gently. Chill overnight. Just before serving fold in reserved 1 Tbsp. lime juice. Makes 5 cups.

## Italian Salsa

1 Tbsp. olive oil
1 cup diced onion
½ cup diced green pepper
1 large clove garlic, minced
½ cup diced Canadian bacon
   or turkey ham
2 cups cooked black beans
1 14.5-oz. can Italian-style diced tomatoes
   with basil, garlic, & oregano
¼ tsp. salt

Heat oil in a medium non-stick skillet. Add onion, green pepper, garlic, and Canadian bacon. Sauté 5 minutes. Remove from heat and add beans, tomatoes, and salt. Stir well. Cover and chill for at least 1 hour before serving. Makes 4 cups.

Variation:  replace cooked black beans with a 19-oz. can of black beans or black-eyed peas, rinsed & drained. Omit salt if using canned beans.

## Black Bean Bruschetta

1 recipe Bruschetta (page 172)
1 cup Black Bean Hummus (page 31)
   or favorite hummus

### Tomato Mixture:
2 medium tomatoes, minced
½ cup thinly sliced green onions (approx. 6
   onions)
1 Tbsp. olive oil
3 Tbsp. chopped fresh basil
Black pepper to taste

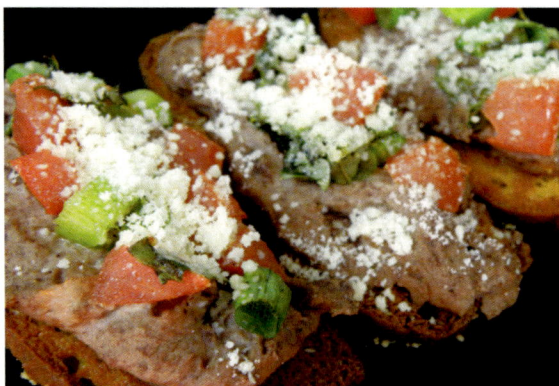

### Topping:
½ cup grated Parmesan cheese

Spread hummus on bruschetta slices. Combine tomato mixture ingredients and spoon on top of hummus. Sprinkle with cheese. Bake at 400º for 4-5 minutes. Serve immediately. Makes 25-30 bruschette.

## Spinach-Artichoke Bruschetta

1 recipe Bruschetta (page 172)

### Topping:
1 6.5-oz. jar marinated artichoke hearts,
   drained & finely chopped
½ cup grated Parmesan cheese
1 large Roma tomato, seeded
   & finely chopped
⅓ cup finely chopped red or sweet onion
⅓ cup finely chopped fresh baby spinach
5 Tbsp. mayonnaise
1 clove garlic, minced

In a bowl, combine topping ingredients. Spread on bruschette. Place onto ungreased baking sheets and bake at 350º for 10 minutes, until hot. These can also be broiled 3-4" from heat for 3-4 minutes or until edges are lightly browned and topping is hot. Serve immediately. Makes 25-30 bruschette.

## BLT Bruschetta

½ recipe Bruschetta (page 172)

**Topping:**
1½ Tbsp. oil
5 slices turkey bacon
½ cup finely chopped & seeded tomato
½ cup finely chopped leaf lettuce
2-4 Tbsp. traditional basil pesto, to taste
¼ tsp. salt
¼ tsp. black pepper

Dice bacon and fry in oil until crisp. Combine topping ingredients. Spread a tablespoonful onto each slice of bruschetta. Serve immediately. Makes 20 bruschette.

## Mozzarella Bruschetta

½ recipe Bruschetta (page 172)

**Topping:**
1 large tomato, seeded & finely chopped
3 Tbsp. minced fresh basil or 1½ tsp. dried basil
⅛ tsp. salt
¼ tsp. black pepper
Mozzarella cheese, sliced (approx. 10 oz.)

In a small bowl, combine tomato, basil, salt, and pepper. Spread a tablespoonful of topping on each slice of bruschetta. Top with a slice of cheese. Spoon another 2 tsp. of topping on top of cheese. Bake at 400° for 5-8 minutes, just until cheese melts. Serve immediately. Makes 20-25. Note: if necessary, drain topping before using.

## Crab Melt Bruschetta

1 recipe Bruschetta (page 172)

**Crab Salad:**
1 8-oz. package imitation crab meat or legs, chopped
¼ cup mayonnaise
2 green onions, thinly sliced
1 stalk celery, diced
1 cup shredded mozzarella cheese
¼ tsp. salt

Chop crab meat in food processor. Pour into bowl and mix with remaining crab salad ingredients. Place bruschetta slices on a baking sheet and top with crab salad. Bake at 350° for 10 minutes or until cheese has melted and crab salad is hot. Makes 30-35 bruschette.

## Fresh Feta Bruschetta

½ recipe Bruschetta (page 172)

**Topping:**
1 large tomato, seeded & finely chopped
1 medium zucchini, finely chopped
4 green onions, thinly sliced
2 Tbsp. minced fresh basil
4 cloves garlic, minced
2 Tbsp. lemon juice
2 Tbsp. olive oil
¾ tsp. salt
¼ tsp. black pepper
½ cup feta cheese

In a large bowl combine tomato, zucchini, onions, basil, and garlic. In a small bowl whisk together lemon juice, oil, salt, and pepper. Pour juice mixture over tomato mixture and toss to coat. Fold in feta cheese. Cover and chill for at least 1 hour. To serve, scoop out topping with a slotted spoon and mound onto bruschetta slices. Serve immediately. Makes 20.

## Hummus & Avocado Bruschetta

1 recipe Bruschetta (page 172)

**Topping:**
1 recipe Red Pepper Hummus (page 36)
1 small red onion, thinly sliced
1 large cucumber, thinly sliced
1 4-oz. or 5-oz. carton of desired sprouts
   (alfalfa, radish, broccoli sprouts, etc.)
2 ripe avocados, pitted, peeled, & thinly sliced

Spread each slice of bruschetta with hummus. Top with onion, cucumber, sprouts, and avocado. Makes 25-35 bruschette.

Variation: try other hummus recipes such as **Greek Parsley Hummus (page 32)**, **Italian Red Feta Hummus (page 36)**, or **Lemon Sage Hummus (page 37)**. Sliced tomatoes also work well on these.

## Chicken and Cheese Quesadillas

**1 recipe of Oat Bran Crackers (page 177)**
**Butter**
**Shredded chicken, leftovers work fine**
**Sliced cheddar cheese**

Make **Oat Bran Crackers** about 3" in diameter. To assemble quesadillas, butter one side of each cracker. Lay buttered side down into a non-stick skillet. Slice cheese to fit crackers. Lay a piece of cheese on cracker, layer chicken next, then a little more cheese, and end with a buttered cracker, butter side up. Fry over medium heat until lightly browned on the bottom. Flip and brown on other side until cheese has melted. Try different kinds of cheese. These are also good as cheese quesadillas simply by leaving off the chicken. Makes 7 quesadillas.

## Tex-Mex Quesadillas

**1 recipe Oat Bran Crackers (page 177)**
**Butter**
**1 15-oz. can black beans, rinsed & drained**
**1 cup shredded carrots**
**1 cup shredded Monterey Jack**
    **or pepper jack cheese**

Make **Oat Bran Crackers** about 3" in diameter. To assemble quesadillas, butter one side of each cracker. Lay butter side down into a non-stick skillet. Slightly mash beans and spread a spoonful on cracker. Top with a spoonful each of carrots and cheese. Place another cracker on top, butter side up, and press slightly. Fry over medium heat, until lightly browned on the bottom. Flip and brown on other side until cheese has melted. To serve, dip in salsa and sour cream. Makes 7 quesadillas.

## Note

There is no end to the variety of possibilities with these quesadillas. Try pepperoni and mushrooms between two slices of mozzarella or provolone cheese; bacon and tomatoes with colby cheese slices; refried beans and pepper jack cheese; or any of your favorite toppings and cheese slices.

## Crab Puffs

1 cup plus 1 Tbsp. water
½ cup butter
1 Tbsp. prepared horseradish
1 tsp. salt
⅛ tsp. red pepper sauce (hot sauce)
1 cup garbanzo bean flour
4 eggs
2 cups shredded Swiss cheese
8-oz. frozen imitation crab legs
  or crab meat pieces, thawed

In a large saucepan, bring water, butter, horseradish, salt, and red pepper sauce to a boil. Add flour all at once and whisk to blend. Remove whisk and stir with a wooden spoon until a smooth ball forms. Remove from heat. Let stand for 5 minutes. Add eggs one at a time, beating well after each. Continue beating with spoon until smooth and shiny. Stir in cheese and crab. Drop by rounded teaspoonfuls 2" apart onto oil-sprayed baking sheets. Bake at 400° for 20-25 minutes, until golden brown. Remove from pans and transfer onto wire cooling racks. Serve warm with **Horseradish Cream Bean Dip (page 47)** that has been thinned with **Almond Milk (page 107)**. These are best eaten right away. They can be refrigerated or frozen and reheated, but will not be as crispy. Makes 25-30 puffs.

## Cajun Black-Eyed Pea Fritters

1¼ cup dried black-eyed peas
4 cups water
1 medium onion, chopped
1 medium chipotle (canned)
  in adobo sauce, seeded
1 tsp. salt
1 tsp. celery salt
1 tsp. Cajun seasoning

Soak black-eyed peas overnight in water. Drain. Briskly rub peas between the palms of hands to remove skins. Return peas to a bowl. Cover peas in water and skins will float to surface. Discard skins and allow peas to soak for 2 hours longer. Drain. Place peas and remaining ingredients into a food processor. Puree until a smooth, thick paste. Heat 1" of oil in a heavy skillet. Drop by teaspoonfuls into hot oil. Fry until golden brown, flipping halfway through. Remove with a slotted spoon and place on a paper-towel-lined plate. Serve with your favorite dipping sauce. Serves 6.

## Sesame Bean Balls

2 cups Cauli-rice (page 168)
1 15.5-oz. can black beans, rinsed & drained
½ cup almonds
1 egg
1 Tbsp. soy liquid aminos or soy sauce
½ tsp. curry powder
½ tsp. garlic powder
1 cup sesame seeds or ground nuts

### Dipping Sauce:
Toasted sesame dressing (purchased)

Place cauli-rice into a large bowl. Puree beans in a food processor and add to bowl. Place almonds in food processor and pulse to a meal, almost a flour. Stir into bean mixture. Add egg, liquid aminos, curry powder, and garlic powder. Mix well. Scoop out balls of mixture using a small trigger-style scoop. Roll in sesame seeds and place onto a large oil-sprayed baking sheet. Bake at 375º for 15 minutes. Serve hot, with Asian dressing. Makes 50.

Variations: for Italian flavor, replace curry with basil or Italian seasoning and dip in spaghetti or marinara sauce. For Mexican flavor, replace curry with taco seasoning or chili powder and dip in salsa or nacho cheese sauce.

## Red Pepper Hummus Deviled Eggs

4 hard-boiled eggs*
1 8-oz. carton roasted red pepper hummus
2 Tbsp. diced tomatoes
2 fresh basil leaves, chopped (optional)

Remove shell from hard-boiled eggs, rinse and dry. Cut eggs in half length-wise, remove yolks or set aside for another use. Fill each half egg with 2 Tbsp. hummus. Top each with tomatoes and basil. Makes 8.

Variation:  replace store-bought hummus with **Red Pepper Hummus (page 36)**, **Tomato Pesto Hummus (page 34),** or other hummus recipe from this book.

* **To hard-boil eggs:** Place eggs in a medium saucepan. Add cold water to at least 1" above eggs. Bring to a boil over med-high heat. Remove from heat, cover, and let stand for 20-24 minutes, depending on size of eggs. Immediately cool eggs in cold water to stop cooking. To peel, tap egg on both ends to crack shell then roll on counter or between hands. Gently peel shell away while holding egg under running water.

## Chili Fritters

1 cup split peas, sorted & rinsed
Water
1 small onion, coarsely chopped
3 large cloves garlic
½ tsp. baking powder
2 tsp. chili powder
¾ tsp. salt
¼ tsp. black pepper
¼ tsp. crushed red pepper flakes

### Dip:
Salsa con queso or nacho cheese sauce

Place dry split peas into a large non-metal bowl and add cool water to cover 2" above peas. Soak in refrigerator overnight. Drain and rinse. Drain well. Place split peas into a food processor and pulse to coarsely chop peas. Add remaining ingredients. Puree until mixture is smooth, scraping sides as needed. Heat 1½-2" of oil in a large skillet (heat oil to 375° if using a deep fryer). Check to make sure oil in skillet is hot by standing the handle of a wooden spoon upright in the oil. When bubbles form around the handle, the oil is ready. Using 2 teaspoons, scoop mixture with one spoon and scrape mixture into hot oil with the other spoon. Fry 6-10 fritters at a time. Do not scoop heaping spoonfuls or fritters will be doughy in the middle. Fry until fritters are a medium brown on one side, then flip to brown other side. Remove fritters with a heat-resistant slotted spoon and place onto a paper towel-lined plate. Serve hot with dip. Heat any brand of salsa cheese sauce (salsa con queso) or nacho cheese sauce.

**Variation:** add 1½-2 cups shredded pepper jack cheese to mixture before frying. For a fluffier fritter, increase baking powder to 1 tsp. Makes about 45 fritters.

## Baked Pumpkin Seeds

2 cups pumpkin or squash seeds
1½ Tbsp. safflower or light olive oil
Salt to taste (plain, garlic, onion
    or celery)

Remove seeds from pumpkin or squash. Separate fiber from seeds, but do not wash; or purchase raw seeds at a bulk food store. Mix seeds with oil and sprinkle with salt of choice. Spread seeds onto 2 oil-sprayed baking sheets. Bake at 300° for 30-45 minutes or until crisp and brown. Stir occasionally. Pour onto waxed paper to cool. Store in a tight container.

**Variation:** replace salt with either 2 Tbsp. Parmesan cheese, 1½ Tbsp. soy liquid aminos, or 1½ Tbsp. soy sauce.

## Spinach Balls

1 regular size loaf of
   Bean Flour Yeast Bread (page 171)
1½ Tbsp. rubbed sage
1 tsp. salt
4 tsp. onion powder
¼ cup melted butter
4 eggs
1 cup grated Parmesan cheese
½ cup water
10-oz. frozen chopped spinach,
   thawed (undrained)

Cube bread and place in a large bowl. Add remaining ingredients, including liquid from thawed spinach. Mix well with hands. Mixture should stick together when pressed into a ball in the palm of hand. Using a small trigger-style scoop, scoop out a ball at a time. Press together to form into 1" balls. Place onto oil-sprayed baking sheets. Bake at 350º for 10 minutes, or until lightly browned on bottoms. Serve with Ranch dressing, curry dip, **Horseradish Cream Bean Dip (page 47)**, or regular yellow mustard. Makes about 70 balls.

Note: this recipe can be used as a substitute for stuffing.

## Roasted Garbanzo Party Mix

7 cups roasted garbanzos (salted or unsalted)
1 cup cashews, halves and pieces
1 cup raw pumpkin seeds (pepitas)

### Sauce
⅔ cup butter, melted
8 tsp. Worcestershire sauce
2 tsp. garlic powder
2 tsp. onion powder
2 tsp. celery salt

In a large bowl combine roasted garbanzos, cashews, and pumpkin seeds. In a small bowl, whisk together sauce ingredients. Pour sauce over garbanzo mixture, using a spatula to scrape out all of the sauce. Stir well to coat. Pour into 2 ungreased 9x13" glass baking pans. Level out. Bake at 250º for 1½ hours. Stir every 20 minutes. Allow to cool in pans. Makes 9 cups of mix.

Variation:  add some broken **Oat Bran Crackers (page 177)** to mix before baking.

Note: Roasted garbanzo beans can be purchased at a natural whole foods store.

25

## Falafel

1 cup dry garbanzo beans,
   sorted & rinsed
½ tsp. baking powder
1 small onion, coarsely chopped
3 large cloves garlic, minced
2 handfuls fresh parsley,
   coarsely chopped
2 tsp. dried basil
¾ tsp. salt
¼ tsp. black pepper
⅛-¼ tsp. crushed red pepper flakes

### Tahini Sauce
½ cup tahini (sesame seed paste)
3 cloves garlic, crushed
½ tsp. salt
2 Tbsp. olive oil
¼ cup lemon juice

Place dry garbanzo beans in a large bowl and cover with cool water to 2" above beans. Soak in the refrigerator for at least 18 hours and up to 24 hours. The beans will swell to triple their original size. Drain and rinse thoroughly. Place beans into a food processor and pulse to coarsely chopped. Add remaining ingredients. Puree until mixture is smooth, stopping and scraping sides several times. Heat 1½-2" of oil in a large skillet. (Heat oil to 375º if using a deep fryer.) Check to make sure oil in skillet is hot by standing the handle of a wooden spoon upright in the oil. If bubbles form around the handle the oil is ready. While oil is heating, scoop out a tablespoonful of falafel at a time. Form into a nugget or ball. Carefully place 8-10 nuggets into oil at a time. Make sure they do not stick to bottom. Fry until falafel fritters are a crusty medium to dark brown on all sides, turning as needed, 3-5 minutes per batch. Remove falafels with a slotted spoon and drain on a platter lined with paper towels. These are good hot or cold. Makes about 25 falafel. Serve with tahini sauce.

To make tahini sauce, combine garlic and tahini in a food processor or with mortar and pestle. Add remaining ingredients and stir. If too thick, add a teaspoon or two of warm water until desired consistency.

Variation: for a more traditional Middle Eastern flavor, when making the falafel replace basil with cumin and parsley with cilantro.

## Garbanzo Nuts

2 15.5-oz. cans garbanzo beans,
   rinsed & drained
2 Tbsp. extra virgin olive oil
1 tsp. garlic salt
1 tsp. onion powder

### Topping:
Garlic salt to taste

Mix together ingredients, except topping, on a baking sheet.  Bake at 400º for 15 minutes.  Reduce heat to 200º and bake 2 hours longer, stirring every ½ hour.  Sprinkle with additional garlic salt. Makes 1½ cups nuts.

## Nutty Lentil Crumbles

2 cups cooked lentils (not mushy)
¾ cup walnuts
3 Tbsp. butter, melted
¼ tsp. thyme
1 Tbsp. soy liquid aminos or soy sauce

Place lentils into a food processor and pulse until almost mashed.  Pour into a bowl.  Place walnuts into food processor and process until ground into small crumbles.  Add to bowl, along with remaining ingredients. Spread out on an oil-sprayed 9x13" casserole dish.  Bake at 350º for 30 minutes.  Remove from oven and chop.  Bake an additional 15-20 minutes.  Mixture should be dry and crumbly.  Eat by the spoonful or use as topping for any casserole or salad.  Makes 1½ cups.

## Stuffed Cherry Tomatoes

1 pint cherry tomatoes
Hummus or bean dip of your choice

Wash and cut the tops off the cherry tomatoes. Scoop out insides.  Fill inside of each cherry tomato with dip.  Set filled tomatoes on a plate. Cover and chill.  **Basil Pesto Spread (page 38), Horseradish Cream Bean Dip (page 47)**--pictured at right, and **Spicy Garlic Hummus (page 35)** all taste good in these.  Makes about 20 tomatoes.

## Bean Peanut Butter Cookies

1 cup peanut butter
½ cup butter, soft
½ cup baked beans, rinsed and drained
2 eggs
1 Tbsp. vanilla
2 tsp. butterscotch flavoring
1½ cups of garbanzo bean flour
1/2 cup of oat bran
1/4 tsp. salt
¾ tsp. baking soda
1/2 tsp. baking powder
1 cup chopped pecans

Cream together peanut butter and butter. Place beans in food processor with eggs and process until smooth. Add to peanut butter mixture. Add the rest of the ingredients in the order given. Mix well. Form into balls with a small size trigger style scoop. Place 2" apart onto an ungreased baking sheet. With a fork dipped into garbanzo flour, make a crisscross indent on each cookie, while flattening them. Bake at 375 degrees for about 10 minutes. Remove to a cooling rack until cooled. Makes 3 dozen.

## Notes

For additional snack ideas try:

**Fry Bread (page 178)**
**Pita Crisps (page 178)**, including **Basil, Onion Dill,** or **Rosemary Pita Crisps**
**Pretzels (page 171)**
**Carrot Muffins (page 181)**
**Carrot Cake (page 181)**
**Pumpkin Muffins** or **Pumpkin Peanut Butter Muffins (page 182)**
**Oat Bran Crackers (page 177)**
**Snack Stix (page 177)**
**Cheesy Egg Puffs (page 99)**
**Funnel Cakes (page 113)**
**Pumpkin Pie (page 163)**

# Hummus, Spreads & Dips

## Black Bean Hummus

1 15-oz. can black beans,
    rinsed & drained
¼ cup chopped onion
2 cloves garlic
2 Tbsp. lime juice
1 Tbsp. Thousand Island dressing
⅛ tsp. salt
¼ tsp. black pepper

Place all ingredients into a food processor and puree until smooth. Makes 1½ cups.

## Tahini Black Bean Hummus

1 15-oz. can black beans,
    rinsed & drained
¼ cup tahini (sesame seed paste)
1 Tbsp. minced garlic
1 Tbsp. extra virgin olive oil
1 tsp. lime juice
½ tsp. cumin

Place all ingredients into a food processor. Puree until smooth. Makes 1½ cups.

## Kidney Bean Hummus

1 15-oz. can red kidney beans,
    rinsed & drained
1 green onion, top only, chopped
1 large clove garlic, minced
¼ tsp. red pepper sauce (hot sauce)
1 tsp. Worcestershire sauce
1½ tsp. lemon juice
1 Tbsp. mayonnaise

Place all ingredients in food processor and puree until smooth, scraping down sides occasionally. Chill before serving. Makes 1½ cups.

## Greek Parsley Hummus

1 15-oz. can garbanzo beans, rinsed & drained
3-4 Tbsp. fresh lemon juice, to taste
½ tsp. dried oregano
    or 1 sprig fresh oregano, chopped
1 clove garlic, minced
¼ tsp. salt
2 rounded Tbsp. tahini (sesame seed paste)
1 handful fresh parsley, without stems
3 Tbsp. water
1 Tbsp. chopped ripe olives

Place all ingredients, except olives, into a food processor and process until smooth. Transfer into a bowl and stir in olives. Serve with cucumbers and sweet red peppers cut into sticks for dipping. Makes 2 cups.

## Layered Greek White Hummus

### Hummus:
1 19-oz. can cannellini beans,
    rinsed & drained
¼ cup sour cream
2 Tbsp. fresh lemon juice
2 Tbsp. tahini (sesame seed paste)
1 tsp. dried dill weed
1 large clove garlic, minced
1 tsp. grated lemon peel
¼ tsp. salt
¼-½ tsp. black pepper

### Toppings:
2 Roma tomatoes, diced
½ cup cucumber, diced
⅓ cup green onion tops, chopped
¼-½ cup crumbled basil and tomato feta cheese
2 Tbsp. chopped black olives

Place all hummus ingredients in food processor. Process until smooth. Spread hummus evenly over the bottom of a 9" or 10" serving plate or pie plate. Place toppings on hummus in order listed. Cover with plastic wrap and chill for at least 1 hour before serving. Serve with green pepper slices and other fresh vegetables. Serves 10.

## Hamburger Hummus

### Hummus:
1 19-oz. can garbanzo beans,
 rinsed & drained
2 cloves garlic, minced
¾ tsp. salt
¼ tsp. crushed red pepper flakes
¼ cup tahini (sesame seed paste)
2 Tbsp. water
2 Tbsp. lemon juice
1 Tbsp. extra virgin olive oil

### Burger:
¼ lb. (½ cup) ground beef
⅛ tsp. ground allspice
⅛ tsp. black pepper
1 tsp. dried chives
¼ tsp. paprika

Place hummus ingredients into a food processor and puree until smooth. Mix burger ingredients together and brown in large skillet. Add hummus to skillet and heat through. Serve in hollowed tomatoes, on green pepper quarters, or on **Bruschetta (page 172)**. Serves 8.

Variation: spread warm hummus on green pepper quarters, top with Monterey Jack cheese, and broil until cheese melts, 5-7 minutes.

## Southern Hummus

1 15-oz. can black-eyed peas,
 rinsed & drained
1 clove garlic
2 green onions (tops & bottoms),
 chopped
1 Tbsp. chopped fresh parsley
3 Tbsp. lemon juice
⅓ cup tahini (sesame seed paste)
½ tsp. salt
¼ tsp. chili powder
1 4-oz. can diced green chilies,
 divided

Place all ingredients into a food processor, except 2 Tbsp. green chilies. Puree until smooth. Fold in remaining chilies. Chill. Makes 2 cups.

## Tomato Pesto Hummus

**1 15-oz. can cannellini beans,**
   **rinsed & drained**
**¼ cup sun-dried tomato pesto**

Place both ingredients into a food processor and puree until somewhat smooth. Chill for a couple of hours. Makes 1½ cups.

Variation: replace cannellini beans with garbanzo beans.

## Sundried Tomato & Roasted Garlic Hummus

**1 whole garlic head**
**1 cup water**
**1 cup sun-dried tomatoes,**
   **packed without oil**
**2 Tbsp. extra virgin olive oil**
**¼ tsp. dried rosemary**
   **or ½ tsp. fresh chopped rosemary**
**¼ tsp. salt**
**¼ tsp. black pepper**
**1 16-oz. can Great Northern beans,**
   **rinsed & drained**

Remove white papery skin from garlic head, but do not peel or separate cloves. Wrap head in foil. Bake at 375° for 45 minutes. Let cool for 10 minutes. Separate cloves and squeeze out garlic pulp. Discard skins. Bring water to a boil in saucepan. Add tomatoes. Cover and remove from heat. Let stand 10 minutes. Drain tomatoes (reserve liquid and add a little only if hummus is too dry). Place all ingredients into a food processor and puree until smooth. Stop and scrape sides and bottom several times. Processing will take several minutes. Let chill and flavors blend overnight. Makes 2 cups.

## Roasted Garlic-Artichoke Hummus

1 head of garlic cloves
1 15-oz. can cannellini beans,
    rinsed & drained
1 12-14-oz. can or jar artichoke hearts
    (not marinated), drained
¼ cup tahini (sesame seed paste)
1 Tbsp. lemon juice
¼ tsp. salt

Remove the white papery covering on the head of garlic cloves.  Wrap the garlic head in aluminum foil and bake at 375º for 45 minutes, or until tender.  Allow to cool 10 minutes.  Slip cloves out of their skins.  Discard skins and place cloves into food processor.  There should be about ⅓ cup roasted garlic cloves.  Add remaining ingredients and process until smooth.  Let hummus chill and flavors blend overnight.  Makes 3 cups.

## Spicy Garlic Hummus

1 14.5-oz. can garbanzo beans,
    rinsed & drained
1 Tbsp. lemon juice,
    or juice from ½ lemon
½ tsp. salt
¼-½ tsp. red pepper flakes
1 clove garlic, chopped
3 Tbsp. extra virgin olive oil

Place beans, lemon juice, salt, pepper flakes, and garlic into a  food processor. Use ¼ tsp. of pepper flakes for mild flavor or ½ tsp. if more heat is desired. Turn on processor and drizzle in oil while processing.  You may need to stop and scrape the sides down several times. Adjust oil, adding more if needed for desired consistency.  Serves 6.

Variation:  for **Spicy Curry Hummus** add 1 tsp. curry powder.

## Italian Red Feta Hummus

½ cup roasted red pepper (from jar)
1 15-oz. can cannellini beans,
    rinsed & drained
1 tsp. dried basil
¼ tsp. garlic powder
1 4-oz. container tomato basil feta
1 Tbsp. extra virgin olive oil

Combine all ingredients in a food processor and process until smooth. There will still be bits of feta in the hummus. Chill for several hours or overnight to let the flavors blend. This hummus is also very good served hot. Makes 2 cups.

## Red Pepper Hummus

⅓ cup mayonnaise
1 Tbsp. lime juice
1 15-oz. can garbanzo beans, rinsed & drained
¼ cup chopped roasted red peppers, drained
1 clove garlic, peeled and coarsely chopped
½ tsp. chili powder
¼ tsp. ground cumin

Combine all ingredients in a food processor and process until smooth. Chill for at least 1 hour. Makes 1½ cups.

Variation: For more garlic taste, add 1 more garlic clove. Be aware that the garlic will get stronger as the hummus sits.

## Lemon Sage Hummus

1 15-oz. can cannellini beans,
    rinsed & drained
¼ cup fresh lemon juice
1 tsp. dried sage or
    1 heaping Tbsp. chopped fresh sage
1 small clove garlic, minced
1½ Tbsp. extra virgin olive oil
¼ tsp. salt
¼ tsp. black pepper

Combine all ingredients in a food processor and puree until smooth. Chill for several hours or overnight to let the flavors blend. Makes 1½ cups.

## Bean and Nut Paté

1 14-oz. can baked beans,
    rinsed & well drained
½ cup chopped pecans or walnuts
    (or ¼ cup of each)
1 tsp. sage

Place all ingredients in a food processor and pulse until blended. Paté will not be smooth, but resemble dry chunky peanut butter. Let chill for flavors to blend. Serve on celery or **Oat Bran Crackers (page 177)**. Makes 2 cups.

## Chickpea Peanut Butter

1 15-oz. can garbanzo beans (chickpeas),
    rinsed & drained
½ cup all natural peanut butter
5 Tbsp. lemon juice
2 green onions, chopped
¼ tsp. dried thyme
½ tsp. salt
⅛ tsp. cayenne pepper

Place all ingredients in a food processor and puree until smooth. Let chill for flavors to blend. Serve on celery or **Oat Bran Crackers (page 177)**. Makes 2 cups.

## Mild Lentil Spread

1 stalk celery, chopped
1 green onion, chopped
1 large carrot, peeled & chopped
2 cups cooked lentils
1 Tbsp. rice vinegar
½ tsp. salt

Place celery, onion, and carrot into a food processor. Pulse until minced. Add remaining ingredients and puree until smooth. Allow flavors to blend a couple of hours, or overnight, in refrigerator. Makes 2½ cups.

## Garlic Cheese Spread

1 8-oz. package cream cheese, softened
1 15-oz. can cannellini beans,
    rinsed & drained
¾ cup cheddar cheese spread
¼ cup unsweetened Almond Milk (page 107) or
    unsweetened soy milk
¼ cup grated Parmesan cheese
1½ tsp. garlic powder
1½ tsp. red pepper sauce (hot sauce)
1½ tsp. Worcestershire sauce

Place all ingredients into a food processor and puree until smooth. Chill. Serve on warm **Italian Breadsticks (page 174), Pretzels (page 171), or Garlic Toast (page 172).** Makes 2½ cups.

## Basil Pesto Spread

1 15-oz. can cannellini beans,
    rinsed & drained
6 Tbsp. basil pesto

Place both ingredients into a food processor and puree until smooth. Let chill for several hours or overnight for flavors to blend. Makes 1¾ cups.

## Sunny Split Pea Spread

¾ cup raw sunflower seeds
1 11.5-oz. can split pea soup
   with ham and bacon, undiluted
½ soup can water
¼ tsp. black pepper
1 Tbsp. soy liquid aminos or soy sauce
2 Tbsp. lemon juice, or more to taste
2 Tbsp. mayonnaise

Grind sunflower seeds in a food processor until crumbly. Add remaining ingredients and process until smooth. Processing will take a while to make spread smooth and not gritty. Chill overnight. Makes 2½ cups.

Variation: replace can of soup and water with 1½ cups homemade pea soup.

For **Sunny Split Pea Deviled Eggs,** mix yolks from hard-boiled eggs with spread (about half and half) and spoon mixture into egg whites.

## Bacon and Bean Dip

3 slices turkey bacon, diced
2 Tbsp. olive oil
3 cloves garlic, minced
⅓ cup water
½ tsp. chicken bouillon paste or ½ cube chicken bouillon*
1 15-oz. can cannellini beans,
   rinsed & drained
¼ cup green onions, chopped
1 Tbsp. lemon juice
½ tsp. red pepper sauce (hot sauce)
⅛ tsp. salt
⅛ tsp. paprika

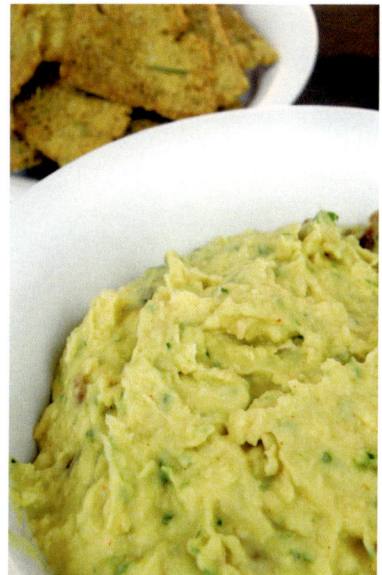

In a small saucepan, cook bacon in olive oil until crisp. Remove bacon with a slotted spoon and set aside. Add garlic to drippings in pan. Cook for 1 minute, stirring frequently. Add water, bouillon, and beans. Stir to dissolve bouillon. Bring to a boil. Reduce heat and simmer, uncovered, for 10 minutes. Combine bean mixture, onions, and remaining ingredients (except bacon) in food processor. Process until smooth. Pour into a bowl and stir in bacon. Serve with **Rosemary Pita Crisps (page 178).** Makes 1½ cups.

Variation: replace 15-oz. can of cannellini beans with a 19-oz. can.

*Better than Bouillon™ is the bouillon paste recommended. If using bouillon cubes reduce or eliminate the salt as bouillon cubes contain more salt than the bouillon paste.

## Hot Baked Artichoke Bean Dip

1 15-oz. can cannellini beans,
    rinsed & drained
1 Tbsp. fresh squeezed lemon juice
1 14-oz. can artichoke hearts, drained
    (not marinated)
1 cup shredded colby jack cheese
½ cup grated Parmesan cheese
½ cup sour cream
⅓ cup mayonnaise
1-2 cloves garlic, minced
1 tsp. Worcestershire Sauce
4 dashes red pepper sauce (hot sauce)
¼ tsp. black pepper

### Toppings:
4 slices of turkey bacon,
    diced & fried crisp
2 Tbsp. chopped green onion tops

Puree cannellini beans and lemon juice in a food processor until smooth. Add artichoke hearts and process until artichokes are chopped finely. Pour mixture into a medium bowl and add remaining dip ingredients, except for toppings. Spread dip into a medium to large casserole dish. Sprinkle toppings over dip. Bake uncovered at 350° for 25 minutes or until mixture is very hot. Allow to cool slightly before serving. Serve with vegetable slices. Serves 15.

Variation: replace colby jack cheese with Swiss cheese.

## Spinach Bean Dip

1 15-oz. can cannellini beans,
    rinsed & drained
1 cup sour cream
1 1.4-oz. envelope vegetable soup mix
¼ cup Almond Milk (page 107)
10-oz. frozen chopped spinach, thawed

Place beans in a food processor and puree until smooth. Add sour cream and puree again. Add soup mix and milk and pulse until blended. Pour mixture into a bowl. Drain spinach then squeeze out excess liquid and pat dry with a paper towel. Stir spinach into the mixture in bowl. Chill for at least 2 hours. Makes 2 cups.

## Easy Mexican Dip

1 16-oz. can mixed beans,
    or pinto beans, rinsed & drained
3 ripe avocados
2 Tbsp. sour cream
1 tsp. lemon juice
1 packet taco seasoning

### Toppings
Diced tomatoes
Grated cheddar cheese
Chopped green onions

In a food processor, puree beans with 1 tsp. taco seasoning mix. Spread onto the bottom of a serving dish or 9x9" glass baking pan. In a food processor puree together avocados, sour cream, lemon juice and remaining taco seasoning. Spread evenly over beans. Garnish with toppings in order given. Serve immediately. Serves 8.

Variation: Dice 2-3 avocados instead of mashing, increase sour cream to ¼-½ cup. Mix sour cream, lemon juice, and taco seasoning together. Gently fold in avocados and layer over beans. Top as before.

## Mexican Bean Burger Dip

1 lb. ground beef
1 medium onion, chopped
1 16-oz. jar salsa (medium or chipotle)
1 15-oz. can refried beans
1 16-oz. can Mexican chili beans
1 16-oz. can black beans,
    rinsed & drained
2 cups shredded cheddar cheese

### Toppings:
Sour cream
Chopped olives (optional)
3-4 Roma tomatoes, diced

Brown ground beef and onion in large skillet or Dutch oven. Drain. Add salsa and beans. Cook until hot. Spread hot dip into 9x13" glass baking dish. Sprinkle with cheese. Bake at 400° for 5 minutes, until cheese melts. Serve with toppings. Serves 8-10.

## Chipotle Salsa Bean Dip

1 16-oz. can refried beans
1 cup chipotle salsa, divided
1 cup shredded sharp cheddar cheese,
    divided
2 Tbsp. chopped green onions

Mix beans, ½ cup salsa, ½ cup cheese, and green onion.  Spread into a glass pie plate.  Spread ½ cup salsa on top of bean mixture.  Top with remaining cheese.  Heat in microwave 3-5 minutes, until dip is heated through and cheese has melted.  Leftovers are also excellent eaten cold.  Makes 2 cups.

## Chicky Guacamole Dip

1 15.5-oz. can garbanzo beans (chickpeas),
    rinsed & drained
2 cloves garlic, minced
1½ Tbsp. lemon juice
½ cup chopped onion
½ avocado, diced
1½ Tbsp. canned diced green chilies
½ tsp. salt
¼ tsp. cayenne pepper
1 cup tomatoes, diced
1 green onion, top only, sliced

Place beans, garlic, and lemon juice into a food processor.  Puree until smooth.  Add onion, avocado, green chilies, salt, and pepper.  Pulse 5-6 times, until mixture is slightly chunky.  Pour into a bowl.
Stir in tomatoes and green onion.  Cover and chill 1 hour before serving.  Store avocado pit in container with dip while chilling to prevent dip from browning.  Discard pit before serving.  Makes 2 cups.

## Creamy Black Bean Dip

1 15-oz. or 19-oz. can black beans,
    rinsed & drained
¾ cup medium salsa
1 large clove garlic, minced
2 Tbsp. mayonnaise
½ tsp. salt

### Topping:
**Shredded Monterey Jack cheese**

Place all ingredients except topping in food processor. Pulse, scraping down sides a couple of times. Dip will not be smooth, but between smooth and coarsely chopped. Place dip into a serving bowl and sprinkle with cheese. Makes 2 cups.

## White Chili Dip or Dressing

1 cup sour cream
1 15-oz. can garbanzo beans,
    rinsed & drained
1 tsp. salt
½ tsp. black pepper
2 green onions, tops only
1 4-oz. can diced green chilies

Place all ingredients into a food processor and puree until smooth. Makes 2½ cups.

## Ranch Chickpea Dip

1 15-oz. can garbanzo beans (chickpeas),
    rinsed & drained
½ cup mayonnaise
    or unsweetened plain yogurt
¼ cup Ranch dressing
2 tsp. lemon juice
½ tsp. cayenne pepper

Place all ingredients into a food processor and puree until smooth. Allow to chill at least 1 hour before serving. Makes 2 cups.

## Quick Hot Party Dip

1 16-oz. can pinto beans, undrained
½ cup shredded cheddar cheese
1 tsp. chili powder
1 tsp. garlic salt
2 tsp. vinegar
2 tsp. Worcestershire sauce
¼ tsp. hickory liquid smoke
2 slices crisply fried turkey bacon, diced

Place beans and their liquid into a food processor and puree until smooth. Pour into a heavy saucepan.
Add remaining ingredients and cook over low heat, stirring constantly, until cheese has melted. For a fancier look, leave out bacon while cooking and sprinkle it on top of dip when serving. Makes 2½ cups.

## Pizza Dip

1 8-oz. package cream cheese, cubed
2 15-oz. jars pizza sauce (without cheese)
1 15-oz. can red kidney beans,
    rinsed & drained
1 6-8-oz. package sliced
    turkey pepperoni, chopped
1 tsp. Italian seasoning
2 cups (8-oz.) shredded mozzarella cheese

Spray a large 5 quart slow cooker. Place cream cheese cubes into the bottom of the slow cooker. In a food processor, puree kidney beans and ⅓ of a jar of pizza sauce until smooth. Place bean mixture into a bowl and add remaining pizza sauce, pepperoni, and Italian seasoning. Spread over cream cheese cubes. Top with mozzarella cheese. Cover and cook on low for 1½-2 hours or until cheese has melted and dip is hot. Serve warm with **Italian Breadsticks (page 174).** Serves 12.

## Hot & Spicy Chorizo Dip

1 lb. ground beef
⅓ lb. uncooked chorizo
½ c. chopped onion
1 packet taco seasoning
2 16-oz. cans refried beans
1 c. shredded Mexican or Monterey Jack cheese
1 11-oz. jar hot salsa
2 c. guacamole
1 c. sour cream
5 green onions, thinly sliced
½ c. minced fresh parsley
¾ c. jalapeno-stuffed olives, sliced, opt.

In a large non-stick skillet, cook ground beef, chorizo, and onion until done. Drain. Stir in taco seasoning. Spread refried beans into an oil-sprayed 9 x 13" casserole dish. In layers, top beans with meat mixture, cheese, and salsa. Cover and bake at 350° for 20-25 minutes, until hot. While still hot, spread guacamole over top. Mix together sour cream, green onions, and parsley. Spread over guacamole. Sprinkle olives over top. Serve immediately. Serves 6-8.

## Peppery Lentil Dip

1 cup dried red lentils,
    sorted & rinsed
2 cups water
¼ cup mayonnaise
¼ cup sour cream
½ tsp. salt
½ tsp. paprika
¾ tsp. cayenne pepper
1 tsp. dry ground mustard

Place lentils and water into a saucepan. Bring to a boil. Reduce heat to a simmer or very low boil. Cook 13-15 minutes, stirring occasionally, until liquid is absorbed. Lentils should be well done, almost mushy. Place lentils and remaining ingredients into a food processor and puree until smooth. Dip may look thin, but will thicken as it sits. For less heat, decrease red pepper to ½ tsp., for more heat use 1 tsp. Serve hot or cold. Makes 2 cups.

Variation:  replace red lentils with green or brown lentils. Increase cooking time to 30-40 minutes. Drain if necessary. The flavor will be the same, but red lentils make a prettier-looking dip.

## Roast Beef 'n' Bean Dip

1 12-oz. can roast beef & gravy
1 11.25-oz. can bean with bacon soup,
    undiluted
1 Tbsp. prepared horseradish

Shred roast beef into a saucepan with gravy. Add bean soup and horseradish. Heat, stirring often. Serve as a dip with **Pita Crisps (page 178),** or spread onto **Bruschetta (page 172),** or **Chickpea Tortillas (page 175).** Serves 4.

## Warm Collard Green Dip

5 slices turkey bacon, diced
2 Tbsp. olive oil
½ medium sweet onion, chopped
2 large cloves garlic, minced
¼ cup water
1 tsp. chicken bouillon paste or 1 cube chicken
    bouillon*
16-oz. frozen chopped collard
    or turnip greens, thawed
8-12 oz. cream cheese, cut into pieces
½ tsp. crushed red pepper flakes
¼ tsp. salt
1 15-oz. can cannellini beans, rinsed,
    drained, & pureed
½ cup grated Parmesan cheese

In a Dutch oven, cook bacon in olive oil until crisp. Remove bacon with a slotted spoon and set aside. Sauté onion and garlic in drippings for 3-4 minutes. Add remaining ingredients, including bacon. Cook, stirring constantly, for 8-10 minutes. Mixture should be hot. Transfer to oil-sprayed 1½ quart baking dish. Bake at 350° for 30-45 minutes, until bubbly. Makes about 4 cups.

Variations: replace frozen collard greens with frozen spinach. Adding extra cheese, such as Swiss cheese is also good.

Serving suggestions: This dip is excellent as stuffing. Try chicken breasts that have been slit and stuffed with dip, sprinkled with a favorite seasoning, and baked at 350° for 1-1½ hours, until chicken is cooked through; or add meat or fish to dip and wrap in cabbage leaves for stuffed cabbage rolls.

*Better than Bouillon™ is the bouillon paste recommended. If using bouillon cubes reduce or eliminate the salt as bouillon cubes contain more salt than the bouillon paste.

## Cheesy Burger Taco Dip

1 lb. ground beef
1 packet taco seasoning
1 16-oz. can pinto beans,
    rinsed & drained
¼ cup cheddar cheese, shredded
½ cup Almond Milk (page 107)

Brown ground beef in a large non-stick skillet. Drain. Mash beans with a fork or potato masher, add taco seasoning and cheese. Stir in **Almond Milk**. Add up to ½ cup more milk if a thinner dip is preferred. Cook over medium heat, stirring constantly. Dip is ready when cheese has melted and dip is heated through. Serve with **Pita Crisps (page   )** or **Garlic Toast (page   )**. Serves 6.

## Horseradish Cream Bean Dip

1 8-oz. package cream cheese
¼ cup prepared horseradish
1 16-oz. can navy or cannellini beans,
    rinsed & drained
½ tsp. salt

Place all ingredients into a food processor and puree until smooth. Serve with vegetable sticks or use as spread for vegetable pizza. Makes 2 cups.

# Salads

## Cajun Lima Bean Salad

**Dressing:**
3 Tbsp. extra virgin olive oil
2 Tbsp. fresh lemon juice
1 Tbsp. Western salad dressing
¼-½ tsp. Cajun seasoning
½ tsp. red pepper sauce (hot sauce)
¼ tsp. Vege Sal® or seasoning salt
1 clove garlic, minced

**Salad:**
1 small sweet red pepper, chopped
1 small red onion, diced
1 medium cucumber, chopped
¼ cup finely chopped fresh parsley
1 15-oz. can small lima or butter beans,
    rinsed & drained

Whisk together dressing ingredients. Start with ¼ tsp. Cajun seasoning and increase to taste. Place all salad ingredients in bowl. Add dressing and toss to coat. Chill. Salad will keep in refrigerator for up to 3 days. Serves 6-8.

## Calico Black Bean Salad

**Salad:**
2 15-oz. cans black beans,
    rinsed & drained
4 green onions, thinly slice whites
    & julienne greens
2 plum tomatoes, chopped
1 large sweet red pepper, chopped

**Dressing:**
2 Tbsp. extra virgin olive oil
2 Tbsp. red wine vinegar
1 Tbsp. lemon juice
½ tsp. salt
¼ tsp. black pepper
¼ tsp. dried basil
    or ¾ tsp. minced fresh basil

In a large bowl, mix together salad ingredients. In a small bowl, whisk together dressing ingredients. Drizzle dressing over salad and toss to coat. Cover and let marinate overnight before serving. Serves 6.

**49**

## Caesar Bean Salad

1 15.5-oz. can garbanzo beans,
   rinsed & drained
2 cups frozen cut green beans, thawed
2 green onion tops, sliced

### Dressing:
⅓ cup Caesar dressing
⅛ tsp. lemon pepper
⅛ tsp. garlic powder

Place beans and onion into a bowl. Whisk together
dressing ingredients and drizzle over bean mixture. Toss to coat. Chill before serving. Serves 4.

## Mustard Bean Salad

### Dressing:
¼ cup safflower or light olive oil
¼ cup apple cider vinegar
2 Tbsp. honey mustard
½ tsp. celery seed
¼ tsp. salt
¼ tsp. black pepper

### Salad:
2 cups frozen cut green bean,
   thawed
1 15-oz. can garbanzo beans,
   rinsed & drained
1 15-oz. can black beans,
   rinsed & drained
1 15-oz. can red kidney or navy beans,
   rinsed & drained
1 cup diced red onions
1 cup diced red, orange or yellow
   bell pepper
⅓ cup chopped fresh parsley

Combine all salad ingredients in a large bowl and mix well. Whisk together dressing ingredients in a small saucepan. Bring to a boil. Remove from heat and pour over salad. Mix in gently. Cover and refrigerate overnight. Stir occasionally. Serves 6-8.

Variation: any or all 15-oz. cans of beans can be replaced with 19-oz. cans.

## Simple Bean Salad

1 15-oz. can black beans,
    drained & rinsed
1 16-oz. can navy or red beans,
    drained & rinsed
1 15-oz. can kidney beans,
    drained & rinsed
1 8-oz. can sliced water chestnuts,
    drained & rinsed
1 handful fresh chives, chopped
Western dressing

Combine all ingredients in a salad bowl, using enough dressing to coat. Chill 1 hour before serving. Serves 6.

## Bean & Gnocchi Salad

1 15-oz. can red kidney beans,
    rinsed & drained
1 15.5-oz. can garbanzo or black beans,
    rinsed & drained
2 cups Gnocchi (page 180)
1 green pepper, chopped
½ cup chopped sweet onion
1 Tbsp. fresh chopped
    or 1 tsp. dried basil
1 Tbsp. fresh chopped
    or 1 tsp. dried thyme leaves

### French Dressing:
2 Tbsp. seasoned rice vinegar
    (not rice salad vinegar)
2 Tbsp. tomato ketchup
½ tsp. paprika
2 tsp. lemon juice
2-3 tsp. chopped sweet onion
¼ cup safflower oil

Combine salad ingredients in a large bowl. Place French dressing ingredients into a blender and blend until smooth. Pour dressing over salad and fold in to coat. Allow to chill several hours for flavors to blend. Serves 8-10.

## Three Bean Raspberry Vinaigrette Salad

1 15-oz. can red kidney beans,
    rinsed & drained
1 15-oz. can black beans,
    rinsed & drained
1 15-oz. can garbanzo beans,
    rinsed & drained
2 green onion tops, sliced
1-2 stalks celery, diced
½ cup raspberry vinaigrette dressing

Combine all ingredients in a salad bowl. Toss and chill. Serves 8.

## Seasoned Italian Salad

### Salad:
1 cup mini carrots, sliced lengthwise
1 cup chopped sweet red pepper
1 cup chopped celery
1 cup diced jicama
1 cup diced zucchini
1 cup small cauliflower florets
½ cup chopped red onion
½ cup sliced green onion tops
1 8-oz. can sliced water chestnuts,
    rinsed & drained
1 15-oz. can black beans, rinsed & drained
1 6-oz. package pepperoni slices, cut in half
1 8-oz. package sharp cheddar cheese,
    diced or cubed

### Dressing:
1 0.7-oz. packet Italian salad dressing mix, dry
¼ cup apple cider or red wine vinegar
3 Tbsp. water
½ cup safflower oil or light olive oil

Place all salad ingredients, except cheese, into a large bowl. Whisk together dressing and drizzle over salad. Toss to coat. Chill at least 1 hour. Add cheese just before serving. Serves 6-8.

Variations: use any vegetables desired—grape tomatoes, broccoli, green and black olives, radishes, etc. Try to use 7-8 cups of vegetables for one recipe of dressing. Bacon bits, nuts, and seeds also work well if sprinkled on just before serving (as with the cheese because they do not store well). Cubed pepperoni sticks or turkey ham can replace pepperoni slices.

## Asian Bean Salad

2 large carrots, peeled and shredded
1 small-medium onion, diced
1 green pepper, diced
1 14-oz. can artichoke hearts, drained
   (not marinated)
1 15.5-oz. can garbanzo beans,
   rinsed & drained
1 15-oz. can red kidney beans,
   rinsed & drained
1 16-oz. can pinto beans,
   rinsed & drained
¾-1 cup purchased toasted sesame dressing
   or a sesame ginger salad dressing

Place carrots, onion, and green pepper into a large bowl. Thinly slice the bottoms of each artichoke until you reach separate layers. Add bottom slices to vegetables. Slice remaining artichoke globes in half lengthwise and julienne layers (about matchstick size) so they separate and resemble little noodles. Add julienned artichokes and beans to vegetables. Shake dressing and fold in ¾ cup to lightly coat salad. Add additional dressing if desired. Chill. Serves 8.

## Moroccan Black Bean and Carrot Salad

1 lb. carrots, peeled and shredded
1 small white onion, sliced very thin
2 Tbsp. olive oil
¼ tsp. crushed red pepper flakes
½ tsp. curry powder (or cumin)
Salt to taste
Black pepper to taste
1 15-oz. can black beans,
   rinsed & drained
2 Tbsp. fresh squeezed lemon juice

In a large pan, sauté onion in hot oil for 2 minutes over high heat, stirring constantly. Onions will begin to caramelize. Add carrots, crushed pepper flakes, curry, salt, and pepper. Sauté for another 2 minutes. Remove from heat and add beans and lemon juice. Stir well. Cool to room temperature before serving. Best if eaten immediately. If made ahead of time, reheat to lukewarm and freshen with a little lemon juice. Serves 6-8.

Variation: for less heat, use only a pinch of red pepper flakes.

## Italian Cauli-cous Salad

### Dressing:
½ cup zesty Italian dressing
2 Tbsp. sun-dried tomato pesto
1 Tbsp. balsamic vinegar
1 Tbsp. freshly squeezed lemon juice
2 tsp. fresh grated lemon peel

### Salad:
1 16-oz. package frozen cauliflower, thawed
1 15-oz. can garbanzo beans, rinsed & drained
1 cup peeled and diced cucumber
1 cup diced orange or yellow bell pepper
1 cup quartered cherry tomatoes
¾ cup chopped green onion tops
½ cup crumbled feta cheese
¼ cup chopped fresh parsley
black pepper to taste

In a small bowl, whisk together dressing ingredients. Chill until ready to use. To make cauli-cous, pulse thawed cauliflower in a food processor until it resembles cous-cous. In a large bowl, toss together cauli-cous and remaining salad ingredients. Pour dressing over salad and mix well. Cover and refrigerate at least 2 hours before serving. Serves 10.

Variation: use cannellini or black beans in place of garbanzos.

## French Bean Salad

1 16-oz. can garbanzo beans, rinsed & drained
1 16-oz. can French-style green beans, drained
1 12-14-oz. can artichoke hearts
     (not marinated), rinsed & drained
     and cut into ⅛'s

### Dressing:
1 0.7-oz. package Italian Dressing, dry
¼ cup red wine vinegar or balsamic vinegar
3 Tbsp. water
½ cup safflower, walnut oil, or light olive oil

Mix together garbanzo beans, green beans, and artichoke hearts. Whisk together dressing ingredients. Pour ½ cup dressing onto salad. Toss gently and chill overnight. Reserve remaining dressing for another use. Serves 6.

## Tuscan Marinated Vegetable Salad

### Dressing:
½ cup of a purchased Tuscan
    or zesty Italian dressing
2 Tbsp. sun-dried tomato pesto
1 Tbsp. balsamic vinegar
1 Tbsp. freshly squeezed lemon juice
2 tsp. freshly grated lemon peel

### Salad:
1 lb.  (1½ cups) fresh green beans,
    cut into thirds
2 cups fresh cauliflower florets,
    cut bite-sized
1 15-oz. can garbanzo beans, rinsed & drained
1 cup (8-oz. jar) stuffed green olives, sliced in thirds
¼ cup thinly sliced sun-dried tomatoes
¼ cup green onion tops, sliced
1 cup halved cherry or grape tomatoes

Mix dressing ingredients and set aside.  Place green beans and cauliflower in a saucepan of boiling water.  Boil for 2-3 minutes, until tender-crisp.  Drain in a colander, rinse under cold water and drain again.  Place in a bowl and add remaining salad ingredients, except tomatoes.  Fold dressing into salad.  Chill 2-3 hours.  Add tomatoes just before serving.  Serves 10-12.

Variation:  Add green beans and cauliflower to salad without boiling them.

## Red & Black Bean Salad

1 15-oz. can black beans,
    rinsed & drained
1 cup diced radishes (about 10)
1 medium tomato, diced
½ cup diced celery
½ cup diced green pepper
½ cup diced sweet onion
½ cup Italian dressing (not zesty Italian)

Combine all ingredients in a bowl. Toss together and chill.  Serves 4-6.

## Mozzo Ball Salad

1 15-oz. can garbanzo beans,
    drained & rinsed
1 pint of grape tomatoes, halved
1 8-oz. container mini mozzarella balls,
    halved
⅓ cup red onion, chopped
⅓ cup fresh basil leaves, chopped
1 Tbsp. extra virgin olive oil
1 Tbsp. balsamic vinegar
1 Tbsp. freshly squeezed lemon juice
½ tsp. salt
¼ tsp. black pepper

In a large bowl, mix all the ingredients in the order given.  Serve immediately or let stand at room temperature for up to 1 hour.  Salad can be made ahead of time and refrigerated if you leave out the tomatoes until just before serving.  Serves 6-7.

Note:  mini mozzarella balls are also called mini bocconcini.  They are sold in the deli department or where specialty cheeses are sold.  They will be in a small cottage cheese style container, covered with water.  Check that the water covers the cheese balls to ensure freshness.

## Balela

1 15.5-oz. can garbanzo beans,
    rinsed & drained
½ can (¾ cup) black beans, rinsed & drained
2 medium tomatoes, seeded, drained,
    and chopped
⅔ cup chopped red onion
½ cup chopped fresh parsley

### Dressing:
3 Tbsp. extra virgin olive oil
2 Tbsp. fresh lemon juice
½ tsp. salt
¼ tsp. garlic powder
Coarse ground black pepper, to taste

To seed and drain tomatoes, cut in half and squeeze halves over sink.  Combine salad ingredients in a large bowl.  Whisk together dressing ingredients and drizzle over salad.  Toss to coat salad.  Let stand for at least 15-30 minutes before serving.  Best served at room temperature.  Keeps well in refrigerator.  Serves 6.

## Garbanzo Cuke Caesar Salad

1 15.5-oz. can garbanzo beans,
   rinsed & drained
1 medium cucumber, quartered & sliced
⅓ cup diced red onion
¼ cup diced sweet red pepper
¼ cup Caesar dressing

Mix all ingredients together in a bowl. Chill 1 hour before serving. Serves 6.

## Bean & Cuke Salad

1 cup chopped green or orange pepper
1 large cucumber, peeled & chopped
½ cup chopped sweet onion
1 clove garlic, minced
1 15-oz. can kidney or black beans,
   rinsed & drained

### Dressing:
½ cup mayonnaise
2 Tbsp. Thousand Island dressing
2 Tbsp. of a purchased honey mustard dressing

In a bowl, mix together peppers, cucumbers, onion, garlic, and beans. Whisk together dressing ingredients and fold into salad. Chill. Serves 6.

Variation: replace beans with baby limas, black-eyed peas, or garbanzo beans. Any of the firmer beans will work.

## Black-eyed Veggie Salad

1 15.5-oz. can black-eyed peas,
   rinsed & drained
1 cup cherry tomatoes, halved or quartered
1 cup shredded carrots
½ cup diced yellow squash or zucchini
½ cup diced red onion
½ cup of a purchased sundried tomato
   vinaigrette with roasted red peppers

Combine all ingredients in a bowl. Toss together and chill. Serves 6.

## Saucy Red Black-Eyed Pea Salad

**Red Dressing:**
2 Tbsp. light olive oil
1 Tbsp. lemon juice
2 Tbsp. Thousand Island dressing
¼ tsp. oregano
2 cloves garlic
2 roasted red pepper halves (from jar)

**Salad:**
1 15.5-oz. can black-eyed peas,
    rinsed & drained
¼ cup diced red onion
⅓ cup diced sweet red pepper
¼ cup feta cheese

Place all dressing ingredients into a blender.  Blend until smooth.  Mix together salad ingredients.
Drizzle dressing over salad and toss to coat.  Serve immediately or chill overnight.  Serves 4.

## Black Bean Salad with Salsa Vinaigrette

**Salsa Vinaigrette:**
3 Tbsp. salsa
3 Tbsp. balsamic vinegar
3 Tbsp. light olive oil
2 tsp. lime juice
2 tsp. Dijon mustard
¼ tsp. salt
1 Tbsp. diced sweet onion or shallots

**Salad:**
1 15-oz. can black beans,
    rinsed & drained
1 medium green, yellow, orange,
    or sweet red pepper, chopped
2 medium fresh ripe tomatoes, chopped
1 stalk celery, diced

Whisk together all vinaigrette ingredients.  Combine salad ingredients in a salad bowl.  Drizzle on
vinaigrette and toss to coat.  Chill for 2 hours or longer before serving.  Serves 8.

## Delicious Refried Bean Salad

1 recipe Delicious Refried Beans (page 150)

### Toppings:
1½ cups shredded lettuce
3 ripe Roma tomatoes, diced
3 Tbsp. diced sweet onion
3 Tbsp. shredded cheddar cheese
3 Tbsp. salsa
3 Tbsp. sour cream

Heat refried beans and divide into 3 salad bowls or plates.  Divide all toppings into 3 portions and layer over beans.  Easy and delicious! Serves 3.

## Southwestern Caviar

1 16-oz. can navy beans, rinsed & drained
1 15-oz. can black beans, rinsed & drained
1 15-oz. can black eyed peas,
   rinsed & drained
1 4-oz. can diced mild green chilies
2 tomatoes, chopped
2 large stalks celery, chopped with leaves
1 medium red onion, chopped
1 large sweet red or orange pepper, chopped
1 clove garlic, minced
⅓ cup white or red wine vinegar
   (or balsamic vinegar)
¼ cup extra virgin olive oil
2 tsp. dried oregano
1 tsp. dried basil
½ tsp. salt

Mix all ingredients together. Allow to marinate in a shallow storage container in refrigerator for 2-5 hours.  Serve with a slotted spoon.  This can be eaten as a salad, as a salsa with **Pita Crisps (page 178)**, or added to other dishes.  Serves 10.

Variation:  replace beans with any beans of choice.  Try pinto beans, red beans, and/or adzuki beans.

## Zippy Southwestern Salad

1 15.5-oz. can garbanzo beans,
    rinsed & drained
1 15-oz. can red kidney beans,
    rinsed & drained
1 15-oz. can black beans,
    rinsed & drained
1 medium red onion, diced
2 stalks celery, diced
1 medium tomato, diced
1 avocado, diced

### Salsa Dressing:
¾ cup thick salsa
¼ cup safflower or light olive oil
1 Tbsp. lemon juice
1 Tbsp. apple cider vinegar
1 tsp. Creole seasoning

Combine all salad ingredients in a large bowl. Whisk together dressing and fold into salad. Chill for at least 2 hours. Serves 8-10.

## Nutty Lentil Salad

1 ½ cups dried green or brown lentils,
    sorted & rinsed
6 cups water
1 sweet red pepper, diced
1 stalk celery, diced
¾ cup chopped pecans
2 Tbsp. chopped parsley

### Dressing:
½ cup sun-dried tomato
    vinaigrette with roasted red peppers

Place lentils and water into a large saucepan. Bring to a boil. Reduce heat and simmer 20 minutes, or until lentils are barely tender. Do not overcook. Drain and rinse in cold water. Place drained lentils and remaining ingredients into a salad bowl. Fold in dressing. Add extra dressing if needed. Chill at least 1 hour before serving. Serves 6-8.

## Red Lentil Salad with Mustard Dressing

2 whole carrots, peeled
1 medium onion, chopped
1 stalk celery, chopped
1 large bay leaf
8 cups water, divided
2 cups dried red lentils
1 medium red onion

### Mustard Dressing:
2 Tbsp. dry ground mustard
1 Tbsp. garbanzo bean flour
½ cup water
6 Tbsp. seasoned rice vinegar
½ cup light olive oil
1 tsp. turmeric
1 tsp. garlic powder
5 tsp. soy liquid aminos or soy sauce

In a medium saucepan combine carrots, onion, celery, bay leaf, and 4 cups water. Bring to a boil, cover, and cook until carrots are tender but not mushy (20-30 minutes). Remove carrots, slice into coins, and set aside. With a slotted spoon, scoop out remaining vegetables and bay leaf from liquid and discard. Pour liquid over lentils in a bowl. If there is not enough liquid to just cover lentils, boil a little more water and add to lentils. Let cool to room temperature. Drain and rinse lentils and transfer to a saucepan. Cover with remaining 4 cups water (or more if necessary to cover lentils). Bring to a boil, reduce heat, and cook for 2-3 minutes, just until tender. Do not overcook or lentils will become mushy. Drain in a colander, rinse with cold water, and drain again. Cut 3 slices from the red onion and set aside for garnish. Chop remaining red onion. In a salad bowl, toss lentils, carrot slices, red onion, and dressing. Whisk together dressing ingredients in a small saucepan over medium heat. Bring to a boil, stirring constantly, and continue cooking until slightly thickened. Cool and toss with salad. Separate onion slices into rings and garnish top of salad. Makes 6-8 servings.

## Fresh Lentil Salad

2 cups peeled, finely diced jicama
1 small tomato, diced
½ cup diced sweet red or orange pepper
¼ cup diced green pepper
½ cup unpeeled diced zucchini
¼ cup diced sweet onion
1 cup cooked lentils
½ cup zesty Italian dressing

Combine all ingredients and chill for 1 hour before serving. Serves 8.

## Lentil Crab Salad

### Salad:
1 8-oz. package imitation
    crab meat or legs, chopped
2 green onions, chopped
1 stalk celery, minced
1 cup frozen peas, thawed & drained
1 cup cooked lentils
1 cup shredded Monterey Jack, cheddar,
    or mozzarella cheese

### Dressing:
½ cup mayonnaise
¼ cup Ranch salad dressing
½ tsp. dried dill weed
Campari tomatoes, small ripe tomatoes,
    or cherry tomatoes

### Garnish:
Dried dill weed

Mix salad ingredients together. Chop crab meat in a food processor. Thaw peas by running hot water over them in a colander. Drain well. Mix together mayonnaise, Ranch dressing, and dill weed. Fold dressing into salad. Cut off tops and hollow out tomatoes. Be sure tomatoes are ripe. Stuff with lentil crab salad and garnish by sprinkling dill weed on top. Campari tomatoes are nice and sweet and just the right size to stuff. Serves 8-10.

## Lentil Egg Salad

3 hard boiled eggs, peeled & rinsed
¾ cup cooked lentils
1 Tbsp. minced onion
3 Tbsp. minced celery
⅓ cup mayonnaise

Place lentils into a food processor and pulse to chop. Chop eggs and add to lentils. Pulse to chop, but do not puree. Pour lentil mixture into a bowl. Add remaining ingredients and mix well. Place on a bed of shredded lettuce, stuff into a hollowed out tomato, or spread onto a piece of **Bruschetta (page 172)**. Serves 4.

## Lentil Chicken Salad

2 cups shredded Romaine lettuce
2 stalks celery, diced
1 large carrot, peeled & shredded
1 cup cooked lentils
1-1½ cups cooked chicken,
    cubed or shredded
½ cup chopped pecans

### Sauce:
1 cup mayonnaise
¼ cup chunky salsa
4 green onions, chopped
1 Tbsp. lemon juice

In a large bowl, combine all salad ingredients. In a small bowl, whisk together sauce ingredients. Pour sauce over salad and stir gently to coat. Serve immediately. If made up ahead of time, store sauce and salad separately and mix just before serving. Serves 6.

## Creamy Kidney Bean Salad

1 15-oz. can red kidney beans,
   rinsed & drained
3 Roma tomatoes, diced
1 stalk of celery, diced
3 green onions, sliced
3 cups shredded romaine lettuce, opt.

### Dressing:
½ cup mayonnaise
¼ cup Ranch salad dressing
1 tsp. dill weed
¼ tsp. garlic powder

In a large bowl, combine beans, tomatoes, celery, and onions. In a separate bowl, whisk together dressing ingredients. Toss salad together with dressing and store in refrigerator for several hours to let flavors blend. If using lettuce, add lettuce just before serving. Serves 6.

## Green Lima-Celery Cups

Lettuce leaves
1 15-oz. can green lima beans,
   rinsed & drained
⅔ cup diced celery

### Dressing:
¼ cup sour cream
1 Tbsp. Almond Milk (page 107)
1 Tbsp. vinegar
1 Tbsp. safflower or light olive oil
1 Tbsp. mayonnaise
¼ tsp. salt
¼ tsp. oregano
⅛ tsp. paprika
1 clove garlic, minced

Line custard cups, ramekins, or teacups with lettuce leaf, torn to size. If cups are not available, use leaves of Bibb lettuce which form their own cups. Combine beans and celery in a bowl. Whisk together dressing ingredients, fold into bean mixture, and toss. Spoon into lettuce cups and sprinkle with additional paprika. Serves 8-10.

## Cool Southwestern Salad

**Salad:**
2 small heads romaine lettuce,
    torn into bite-size pieces
1 15-oz. can pinto beans,
    rinsed & drained
2 avocados, chopped
½ red onion, thinly sliced
½ cup chopped fresh parsley or cilantro

**Dressing:**
¼ cup extra virgin olive oil
¼ cup fresh lime juice
½ tsp. ground cumin
¾ tsp. salt
¼ tsp. black pepper

In a large bowl, combine salad ingredients. In a small bowl, whisk together dressing ingredients. Drizzle dressing over salad and toss to coat. Serve immediately. Serves 10.

## Kidney Bean & Bacon Salad

1 16-oz. can red kidney beans,
    rinsed & drained
6 slices turkey bacon,
    diced & fried crisp
1 cup diced celery
2 hard boiled eggs, diced
½ cup diced dill pickles

**Dressing:**
⅓ cup mayonnaise
2 Tbsp. lemon juice
1 Tbsp. minced onion
Salt to taste
Black pepper to taste

Mix together all ingredients. Chill for several hours. Serves 8.

Variation: add ½ cup diced sweet red pepper or frozen peas (thawed).

## Cottage Tomatoes

1 16-oz. can large butter beans,
    rinsed & drained
½ cup small curd cottage cheese
¼ tsp. onion powder
⅛-¼ tsp. salt, to taste
¼ tsp. black pepper
1 Tbsp. dried chives
4-6 ripe tomatoes
Shredded romaine lettuce

### Garnishes:
Fresh chives
Dried dill weed
Finely chopped walnuts

Puree beans in food processor, scraping down sides often.  Combine bean puree, cottage cheese, onion powder, salt, pepper, and chives.  Cut tops off of tomatoes and hollow out centers.  Fill tomatoes with bean mixture.  Decorate with garnish of your choice.  Chill.  Serve nestled in a bed of shredded lettuce.  Serves 6.

## Curried Black Bean Slaw

⅓ cup mayonnaise or sour cream
2 Tbsp. lemon juice
½ tsp. curry powder
Pinch of salt
1 15-oz. can black beans,
    rinsed & drained
1 cup shredded cabbage
1 cup shredded carrots
¼ cup diced sweet red pepper

In a bowl, mix mayonnaise or sour cream, lemon juice, curry powder, and salt.  Add beans, cabbage, carrots, and red pepper. Toss well.  Cover and chill overnight.  Serves 4-6.

## Sub Salad

6 cups shredded cabbage
1 15.5-oz. can garbanzo beans,
   rinsed & drained
1 cup cubed turkey salami
1 cup cubed colby
   or cheddar cheese
½ cup diced sweet red pepper
¼ cup diced red onion
½ cup diced tomatoes

### Dressing:
½ cup mayonnaise
1 Tbsp. apple cider vinegar
1 Tbsp. light olive oil
1 tsp. prepared yellow mustard
¼ tsp. garlic powder
¼ tsp. black pepper
1-2 Tbsp. Almond Milk (page 107)

Combine salad ingredients in a large bowl. Whisk together dressing ingredients and fold into salad. Chill. Serves 10.

Variation: add banana peppers, cucumbers, or anything found on a sub sandwich.

## Taco Salad

1 lb. ground beef
2 tsp. taco seasoning
1 8-oz. package shredded cheddar
   cheese
1 15-oz. can black beans, rinsed
   & drained
2 tomatoes, chopped
½-1 small sweet onion, chopped
1 large head romaine lettuce,
   washed and torn into bite-size
   pieces
2 avocados, chopped (optional)
1 cup Thousand Island dressing
Taco sauce to taste

Brown ground beef and drain. Add taco seasoning. Mix well and let cool. Mix ground beef, cheese, beans, tomatoes and onions. Chill until ready to eat. Just before serving add lettuce, avocados, and dressing. Add taco sauce to taste. Serves 10. Variation: brown onion with ground beef or replace sweet onion with 1 bunch of green onion tops, sliced.

## Tossed Chickpea Salad with Mellow Dressing

**Salad:**
4 cups romaine lettuce, cut into ribbons
1 cup hickory smoked turkey (from deli),
   or turkey ham, cubed
1 15.5-oz. can garbanzo beans (chickpeas),
   rinsed & drained
½ cup diced sweet or red onion
1 cup diced celery
2 hard boiled eggs, quartered & sliced

**Dressing:**
½ cup mayonnaise
2 Tbsp. Almond Milk (page 107)
1 ½ tsp. prepared horseradish
½ tsp. dry ground mustard

Combine all salad ingredients in a large bowl. Whisk together dressing ingredients. If making ahead, store salad and dressing separately in refrigerator. Toss together just before serving. Serves 4.

## Peas 'n' Peas Salad

1 15-oz. can garbanzo beans (chickpeas),
   rinsed & drained
1 10-oz. package frozen peas, thawed
1 cup celery, chopped
¼ cup diced red onion
1 cup dry roasted peanuts
6 slices turkey bacon, diced & fried crisp
½ cup Western dressing
¼ cup mayonnaise

In a large bowl, mix together chickpeas, peas, celery, onion, peanuts, and bacon. Whisk together dressing and mayonnaise. Fold dressing into salad. Chill. Serves 6.

**Variation:** replace Western dressing and mayonnaise with Caesar dressing. or any dressing of choice.

## Luncheon Bean Salad

2 cups cut fresh green beans
2 cups cut yellow beans
1 medium onion, quartered &
   thinly sliced
⅓ cup diced green pepper
1½ cups finely cubed turkey ham
1 2-oz. jar pimentos, drained
   & squeezed out
1 15-oz. can green lima beans,
   rinsed & drained
1 15-oz. can kidney beans,
   rinsed & drained
1 15.5-oz. can black-eyed peas,
   rinsed & drained
1 cup dressing (Italian, Caesar, etc.)
1 8-oz. package sharp cheddar
   or Monterey Jack cheese, cubed

Place green and yellow beans into a saucepan and cover with water.  Bring to a boil and cook until tender-crisp.  Do not overcook.  Strain in a colander and rinse with cold water.  Transfer to a large bowl.  Add remaining ingredients, except cheese.  Stir well.  Chill.  Add cheese just before serving, Serves 12.

# Turkey Salad Filled Puffs

## Puffs:
1 stick butter
1 cup water
1 cup garbanzo bean flour
1 tsp. onion powder
¼ tsp. salt
1 Tbsp. prepared horseradish
4 eggs
½ tsp. baking powder

## Turkey Salad:
1 cup finely chopped turkey
¼ cup chopped black olives
2 Tbsp. minced onion
2 hard boiled eggs, diced
Dash celery salt
¼ tsp. curry powder
1½ tsp. lemon juice
½ cup mayonnaise

Place butter and water into a medium saucepan. Bring to a boil and boil until butter melts. Have ready: bean flour, onion powder, salt, and horseradish. Add all at once to butter and water, while continuing to cook. Whisk vigorously until mixture is smooth and forms a ball that does not separate. Remove from heat. Allow mixture to cool slightly (a couple of minutes). Add eggs one at a time, beating vigorously after each egg. Beat in baking powder and continue beating until smooth. Drop batter onto an oil-sprayed baking sheet, making 8-10 puffs. For appetizer-sized puffs, drop by heaping teaspoonful. Bake at 400° for 25-30 minutes for large puffs, 20-25 minutes for small puffs, until slightly puffed, golden brown, and dry. Cooking times will vary depending on size, so watch closely. Remove from pan. Let cool. Mix together turkey salad ingredients. Chill if not using right away. Carefully cut off tops of puffs, remove a little of the soft center if necessary, and stuff with turkey salad just before serving. Serves 8-10.

Variation: stuff puffs with your favorite chicken, tuna, or crab salad.

## Thai Turkey Salad

**Salad:**
1 16-oz. can garbanzo beans,
    rinsed & drained
½ tsp. powdered chicken bouillon or broth
1 Tbsp. soy liquid aminos or soy sauce
4 cups mixed greens
1 cup fresh bean sprouts
1 cup cucumbers, unpeeled,
    scored, and thinly sliced
¾ lb. hickory smoked turkey breast
    julienned
½ cup chopped peanuts

**Dressing:**
¼ cup seasoned rice vinegar
2 Tbsp. safflower or walnut oil
1 Tbsp. chopped fresh parsley
1 tsp. lime juice
1 tsp. soy liquid aminos or soy sauce
⅛ tsp. purchased red pepper sauce (hot sauce)

Mix together garbanzo beans, powdered chicken broth, and soy sauce to marinate (about 15 minutes) while preparing the rest of the salad. Drain beans from marinade when ready to assemble salad. Layer salad ingredients in order given in a 9x13" casserole dish. Whisk together dressing ingredients. Drizzle dressing over individual salads just before serving. Serves 8.

## Western Tuna & Bean Salad

1 15.5-oz. can cannellini beans,
    rinsed & drained
1 14.5-oz. can cut green beans,
    well drained
1 6-oz. can tuna, drained
½ small red onion, quartered
    & very thinly sliced
1 cup cherry tomatoes, halved
1 Tbsp. chopped fresh parsley, optional
Western dressing

In a salad bowl combine cannellini beans, green beans, tuna, onion, tomatoes, and parsley if using. Toss with dressing just before serving.

**Variation:** replace tuna with ½ can salmon, drained and deboned. Serves 6-8.

**71**

## Marinated Italian Turkey Tossed Salad

1 16-oz. can pinto beans,
    rinsed & drained
1 15-oz. can kidney beans,
    rinsed & drained
1 15.5-oz. can garbanzo beans,
    rinsed & drained
¼ cup (2-oz. jar) chopped pimientos,
    drained
2 green onions, sliced, tops & bottoms
1 cup cubed cooked turkey breast
6 cups romaine lettuce,
    cut into ribbons

### Dressing:
1 cup spaghetti sauce
⅓ cup red wine vinegar
2 Tbsp. light olive oil

Combine all salad ingredients, except lettuce.  Whisk together dressing ingredients and drizzle over salad mix (less lettuce).  Toss to mix.  Chill for several hours or overnight.  Add lettuce and toss to mix before serving.

Variation:  add 1 chopped sweet red pepper with lettuce.

## Mediterranean Tuna Salad

8-10 cups romaine lettuce
1 medium cucumber, sliced
1 12-oz. can tuna or 15-oz. can salmon,
    drained
1 16-oz. can navy or black beans,
    rinsed & drained
8 cherry tomatoes, halved
½ cup crumbled feta cheese
¼ cup sliced or chopped black olives
4 slices red onion, separated into rings
½ cup Caesar dressing

Divide all ingredients into 4 parts.  Layer in order given into 4 large bowls.  Serve immediately. Makes 4 large individual salads.

## Pesto Tuna and Chickpea Salad

1 15.5-oz. can garbanzo beans (chickpeas),
    coarsely chopped
½ 12-oz. jar roasted red peppers,
    drained & thinly sliced
1 stalk celery, diced
2 6-oz. cans tuna, drained
5 Tbsp. basil pesto
¼ tsp. salt
⅛ tsp. black pepper

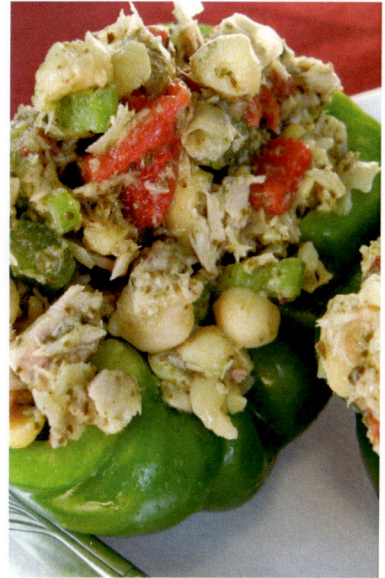

Combine all ingredients in a large bowl.  To eat cold, eat as is, or spread on top of **Oat Bran Crackers (page 177),** or stuff into green pepper halves or small tomatoes.  To eat hot, top **Oat Bran Crackers** with tuna salad and cheese, and broil or bake until cheese melts.  Salad can also be used with **Oat Bran Crackers** to make **Quesadillas (page 21).**  Makes 4 cups.

## Salmon & Kidney Bean Salad

1 7.5-oz. can red or pink salmon,
    drained, deboned, & skinned
2 Tbsp. diced onion
¼ cup diced celery
1 15-oz. can kidney beans,
    rinsed & drained

**Dressing:**
2 Tbsp. lemon juice
1 tsp. prepared yellow mustard
2 Tbsp. Western dressing

Break salmon into bite-sized pieces.  In a small bowl, toss  together salmon, onions, celery, and beans.  In another  small bowl whisk together lemon juice, mustard, and Western dressing. Gently toss dressing with salmon mixture. Chill before serving.  Serves 2-4.

# Soups & Stews

## Quick 'n' Easy Black Bean Soup

1 cup water
1 Tbsp. powdered chicken broth or bouillon
1 15-oz. can black beans, rinsed & drained
½ cup salsa (mild, medium, or hot)
1 12-oz. can chicken breast, drained
1 15-oz. can diced tomatoes

Mix all ingredients in a soup pot. Cook and stir gently until hot. For thicker soup, puree beans before adding to soup. Serves 3-4.

## Kielbasa Bean Soup

1 15-oz. can black beans, rinsed & drained
1 15-oz. can red kidney beans,
    rinsed & drained
1 16-oz. can navy beans, rinsed & drained
2 14.5-oz. cans diced tomatoes, undrained
2 medium green peppers, chopped
2 medium onions, chopped
2 stalks celery, chopped
1 medium zucchini, peeled & diced
4 cloves garlic, minced
4½ cups water
2 tsp. chicken bouillon paste or 2 cubes chicken
    bouillon*
2½ tsp. chili powder
2½ tsp. basil
1 tsp. oregano
1½ tsp. salt
½ tsp. black pepper
2 medium bay leaves
1 ring (16-oz.) smoked beef kielbasa
    or smoked beef polish sausage

In a Dutch oven or large soup pot, mix together all ingredients, except kielbasa or sausage. Bring to a boil. Reduce heat to a simmer. Cover and simmer for 1 hour. Cut kielbasa or sausage in half lengthwise, then cut into ¾" slices. Add to soup and heat through. If kielbasa or sausage is overcooked it will lose its flavor. If making soup ahead of time, remove soup from heat, add kielbasa or sausage, and chill. Reheat and serve. Makes 3 quarts and serves 12.

*Better than Bouillon™ is the bouillon paste recommended. If using bouillon cubes reduce or eliminate the salt as bouillon cubes contain more salt than the bouillon paste.

## Black Bean and Pumpkin Stew

1 medium onion, chopped
1 medium sweet yellow pepper, chopped
1 medium zucchini, peeled & diced
3 cloves garlic, minced
2 Tbsp. olive oil
3 cups water
1 Tbsp. chicken bouillon paste or 3 cubes chicken bouillon*
2 15-oz. cans black beans, rinsed & drained
3 cups cubed cooked turkey or chicken breast
1 15-oz. can solid-pack pumpkin
1 14-oz. can diced tomatoes, undrained
2 tsp. dried parsley
2 tsp. chili powder
1½ tsp. dried oregano
½ tsp. ground cumin

Heat oil in a large non-stick skillet. Sauté onion, yellow pepper, zucchini, and garlic until tender. Pour into a 5 quart slow cooker and stir in remaining ingredients. Cook on low for 4 hours. Makes 2½ quarts.
*Better than Bouillon™ is the bouillon paste recommended. If using bouillon cubes recipe will be saltier.

## Smoked Sausage Stew

1 lb. combination of parsnips, turnips,
     rutabagas, or zucchini, peeled & diced
3 medium carrots, peeled & diced
1 medium onion, chopped
2 15-oz. cans green beans, undrained
1 15-oz. can pinto beans, rinsed & drained
1 tsp. beef bouillon paste or 1 cube beef
     bouillon*
14-16 oz. beef smoked sausage, sliced
2 Tbsp. butter

Place pinto beans and some of the liquid from green beans into a food processor. Puree until smooth. Put vegetable combination into an oil-sprayed 5 quart slow cooker. Add carrots, onion, green beans and remaining liquid, pureed beans, and bouillon. Stir well. Layer sausage slices on top and dot with butter. Do not stir. The sausage will brown nicely on top. Cook on low for 6 hours, or on high for 4 hours, or until vegetables are tender but not mushy. Stir sausage into vegetable mixture just before serving.
Variations:  add another can of pureed pinto beans and 2-3  tsp. of bouillon. Beef or turkey kielbasa or ring bologna can be substituted for the smoked sausage.

*Better than Bouillon™ is the bouillon paste recommended. If using bouillon cubes recipe will be saltier.

## Creole Chicken Soup

4 boneless, skinless chicken breasts
1 cup dry lentils, rinsed
½ cup chicken broth powder
2 quarts water
2 16-oz. cans diced tomatoes
2 cups shredded cabbage
4 stalks celery, chopped
2 small-medium zucchini, peeled & diced
2 large onions, chopped
1 tsp. curry powder
1-2 tsp. Creole seasoning
2 Tbsp. lemon juice
Salt to taste

Slowly cook chicken breasts in enough water to cover them well. Bring water to a boil and cook over medium heat for 45 minutes, or until done. Remove chicken and cut into bite-size cubes (about 4 cups). Set aside. Discard cooking water. In a large soup pot, cook lentils in water and chicken broth powder for 30 minutes. When lentils are done, add vegetables, curry powder, and Creole seasoning. Start with 1 tsp. Creole seasoning and add more for more heat. Cook until vegetables are tender. Add lemon juice and chicken. Heat through. Salt to taste. Serves 10-12.

Variation:  4 cups of cubed turkey leftovers will work well also.

## Chipotle Split Pea Soup

1 Tbsp. olive oil
1 medium onion, chopped
3 carrots, chopped
2 cloves garlic, minced
6 cups water
7 tsp. vegetable bouillon paste or 5 cubes
    vegetable bouillon*
1 cup dried green split peas, rinsed & sorted
1 tsp. canned chipotle pepper in adobo sauce,
    seeded & finely minced
1 8-oz. can tomato sauce

Heat oil in a Dutch oven and add onion, carrots, and garlic. Sauté over medium heat for 5 minutes, stirring often. Add water, bouillon, and peas. Continue cooking for 20 minutes. Add chipotle pepper and tomato sauce. Simmer for 20-30 minutes, until peas are tender. This soup is not as thick as a traditional pea soup. Serves 4-6.
Variation:  add 1 tsp. chili powder for more chili flavor.

*Better than Bouillon™ is the bouillon paste recommended. If using bouillon cubes soup will be saltier.

## Slow Cooker Yellow Split Pea Soup

1 lb. (2 ⅔ cups) dried yellow
   split peas, sorted & rinsed
2 cups sliced baby carrots
2 cups diced celery
1 ½ cups chopped onion
2 cloves garlic, minced
1 large bay leaf
½ tsp. salt
½ tsp. black pepper
6 cups chicken broth
1 large smoked turkey leg

In a 6-7 quart slow cooker, layer ingredients in order given. Bury turkey leg in the center. Do not stir. Cook on high for 4-5 hours or on low 8-10 hours, until peas are very soft and smoked turkey falls off the bone. Remove turkey leg, pull meat off of bone, and discard skin and bone. Cube meat and return to soup. Remove bay leaf before serving.

**Variation:** replace chicken broth with 6 cups of water and 2 Tbsp. chicken bouillon paste or 6 cubes chicken bouillon.*

*Better than Bouillon™ is the bouillon paste recommended. If using bouillon cubes reduce or eliminate the salt as bouillon cubes contain more salt than the bouillon paste.

## Incredible Pea Soup

1-2 smoked turkey legs
9 cups water
3 large carrots, chopped
3 stalks celery, chopped
1 large sweet onion, chopped
2–2 ½ cups dried green split peas,
   sorted & rinsed
1 tsp. oregano
1 tsp. thyme
½ tsp. basil
2 tsp. salt

Combine all ingredients in a Dutch oven or soup pot. Bring to a boil, reduce heat, and simmer for 1½ hours. Remove turkey legs. Pull meat from bones, discard skin and bones, and cut meat into bite-size pieces. Place soup into a blender in batches and blend until smooth. Return soup to pot and add meat. For a thinner soup, use 2 cups dried split peas, for a thicker soup use 2½ cups. Use two turkey legs for a meaty soup, or one if less meat is preferred. Serves 8-10.

## Red Lentil Chili

1¾ cups dried red lentils
4 cups water
1½ tsp. salt
1 lb. ground beef
1 large onion, chopped
3 stalks celery, chopped
1 small jalapeño pepper, seeded & diced
1 4-oz. can diced green chilies
1 14.5-oz. can "chili ready" diced tomatoes
1 10.75-oz. can tomato soup, undiluted
1 Tbsp. chili powder
1 tsp. garlic powder

Place lentils, water, and salt into a large saucepan. Bring to a boil. Reduce heat and simmer 20 minutes. Meanwhile, in a Dutch oven, brown ground beef with onion, celery, and jalapeño pepper until vegetables are very tender. Drain ground beef mixture if necessary. Add remaining ingredients, including lentils and their liquid to chili. Stir well and heat through. Serves 6-8.

Note: red lentils will cook in only 20 minutes. They become mushy and thicken chili well. Brown or green lentils will need to cook for 50 minutes and will not mush as well.

## Peasant Lentil Stew

¼ cup butter
1 large onion, chopped
2 large carrots, peeled & diced
2 stalks celery, diced
2 cloves garlic, minced
1 bay leaf
1 tsp. oregano
1 tsp. basil
2 Tbsp. chicken bouillon paste or 6 cubes
    chicken bouillon*
1 14.5-oz. can crushed tomatoes
8 cups water
2 cups dried lentils, sorted & rinsed
1 cup fresh spinach, washed & thinly sliced
    to resemble fettuccini

Heat butter in a Dutch oven or large soup pot, over medium heat. Add onion, carrots, celery, and garlic and sauté until onion is tender. Stir in bay leaf, oregano, basil, and bouillon. Add tomatoes, water, and lentils. Bring to a boil. Reduce heat and simmer for 1 hour, stirring occasionally. Turn heat off, remove bay leaf, and stir in spinach. Allow spinach to wilt. Soup will thicken into a stew as it stands. Serve with shredded Parmesan or a dollop of sour cream. Serves 10-12.
*Better than Bouillon™ is the bouillon paste recommended. If using bouillon cubes stew will be saltier.

## Smokey Red Lentil Soup

**Stock:**

1 large smoked turkey leg
3 quarts water

**Soup:**

1 cup dried red lentils
1 tsp. baking soda
1 Tbsp. butter
4 carrots, diced
3 stalks celery, diced
2 medium sweet onions, chopped
2 quarts smoked turkey stock
2 Tbsp. vegetable bouillon paste or 6 cubes vegetable bouillon*
Meat from smoked turkey leg

Place turkey leg and water into a soup pot. Bring to a boil and let simmer for 2 hours, or until meat falls off bone. Strain and save broth and set aside. Remove meat from bones and reserve for soup. Rinse lentils in a colander and place in soup pot. Add enough water to cover lentils by about 1 inch. Add baking soda and bring just to a boil. Watch or lentils will easily boil over. Remove from heat and drain and rinse lentils again. In the soup pot, sauté carrots, celery, and onion in butter until they are tender-crisp. Add lentils and smoked turkey stock. Add bouillon and mix well to dissolve. Cook on low for 25 minutes. Add smoked turkey meat and cook another 10 minutes or until lentils are tender but not mushy. Serves 12-14.

*Better than Bouillon™ is the bouillon paste recommended. If using bouillon cubes soup will be saltier.

## Peppery Lemon Lentil Soup

1 ¾ cups lentils, sorted & rinsed
1 parsnip, peeled & chopped
1 carrot, peeled & chopped
10 cups water
5 tsp. beef bouillon paste or 5 cubes beef
    bouillon*
2 Tbsp. olive oil
1 medium onion, chopped
3 large cloves garlic, minced
1 tsp. salt
½ tsp. black pepper
3 tsp. lemon pepper
3 Tbsp. fresh lemon juice
4 cups fresh spinach, cut into ribbons

In a Dutch oven or large soup pot, combine lentils, parsnip, carrot, water, and bouillon. Bring to a boil. Reduce heat, cover, and simmer for 45 minutes. Heat oil in a non-stick skillet over medium heat. Sauté onion and garlic for 5 minutes and add to lentil mixture. Stir in remaining ingredients. Simmer for 5 minutes, until spinach is wilted. Serves 6-8.

*Better than Bouillon™ is the bouillon paste recommended. If using bouillon cubes reduce or eliminate the salt as bouillon cubes contain more salt than the bouillon paste.

# Italian Chili--Pasta e Fagioli

## Seasoned Beef:
1½ tsp. olive oil
1 lb. ground beef
½ tsp. oregano
½ tsp. sweet basil
½ tsp. salt

## Soup:
1½ tsp. olive oil
1 medium onion, chopped
½ lb. carrots, shredded
1 cup celery, diced
24-oz. canned, diced tomatoes
1 15-oz. can black beans, rinsed
1 15-oz. can small white beans, rinsed
1½ tsp. sweet basil
1½ tsp. oregano
1 tsp. garlic powder
1¼ tsp. black pepper
2½ Tbsp. fresh parsley, chopped
1½ quarts beef stock
24-32-oz. spaghetti or tomato sauce

## Topping:
Shredded Parmesan cheese

For beef, place olive oil in 8-10 quart heavy soup pot.  Mix remaining Seasoned Beef ingredients and brown in hot oiled pan, crumbling while cooking.  Remove from pan and set aside.   For soup, add olive oil to pot and sauté onion, celery, and carrots until tender-crisp.  Add remaining soup ingredients and seasoned beef.  Bring just to a boil, reduce heat and let simmer 45 minutes.  Top each bowl with 1-2 Tbsp. Parmesan cheese.  Serves 8-10.

## Chili

1 lb. ground beef
½ large onion, chopped
5 stalks celery, chopped
2 cloves garlic, minced
1 Tbsp. chili powder
¾ Tbsp. salt
3 quarts tomatoes, chopped (4 15-oz. cans)
½ can condensed tomato soup
16 oz. can kidney beans, undrained, divided

### Optional Topping:
Sour cream
Shredded cheddar cheese

Brown ground beef and drain. Add remaining ingredients, except half can kidney beans. Puree the other half can of beans in a food processor or blender, using a little juice from tomatoes if necessary. Simmer on medium heat for approximately one hour, stirring occasionally. Serves 6-8.

Variation: Add two cans of beans rather than one.

## Ranch Chili

### Chili:
2 lbs. ground beef
1 med. onion, chopped
2 15-oz. cans kidney beans, rinsed & drained
2 16-oz. cans pinto beans, rinsed & drained
2 15-oz. cans black beans, rinsed & drained
1 14.5-oz. can diced tomatoes, undrained
1 14.5-oz. can diced tomatoes with green chilies, undrained
1 11.5-oz. can V8 Juice®
2 1-oz. packages ranch salad dressing mix, dry
2 1¼-oz. packages taco seasoning mix, dry

### Optional Topping:
Sour cream
Shredded cheddar cheese

Brown ground beef and onion. Drain. Pour into a 5-quart slow cooker. Stir in remaining ingredients, except toppings. Cover and cook on high for 4 hours. Serve, topped with sour cream and shredded cheese, if desired. Serves 10.

## White Chili

1 Tbsp. extra virgin olive oil
1½ lbs. or 4 boneless, skinless
   chicken breasts, cut into 1" cubes
1 cup chopped sweet onion
1½ cups diced celery
2 cloves garlic, minced
4 tsp. chili powder
1 tsp. cumin
1½ tsp. oregano
½ tsp. coriander
¼ cup garbanzo bean flour
3 cups water
3 tsp. chicken bouillon paste or 3 cubes chicken
   bouillon*
1 14-oz. can evaporated milk
3 15-oz. cans navy beans,
   rinsed & drained
1 4.5-oz. can diced green chilies
½ tsp. salt
½ tsp. black pepper
1 cup sour cream
2 Tbsp. fresh parsley, chopped

### Topping:
**Shredded Monterey Jack cheese**

Heat oil in a large soup pot or Dutch oven over medium-high heat. Add chicken and cook 3-4 minutes, until no longer pink, stirring occasionally. Add onions, celery, and garlic. Cook until vegetables begin to soften, about 5 minutes. Add chili powder, cumin, oregano, and coriander to chicken and mix well. Add flour and stir until chicken is well coated. Stir bouillon into water and add to chicken. Mix well while cooking over low heat. Add evaporated milk. Bring mixture to a boil and reduce heat to a simmer. Simmer uncovered for 5 minutes, stirring occasionally. Scrape bottom while stirring. Add navy beans, green chilies, salt and pepper. Cover and continue to simmer on low for 15 minutes, stirring often. Remove from heat. Stir in sour cream and parsley. Ladle into bowls and top with cheese. This is best made up a couple of hours ahead of time to let the flavors blend. Reheat to serve. Serves 8.

*Better than Bouillon™ is the bouillon paste recommended. If using bouillon cubes reduce or eliminate the salt as bouillon cubes contain more salt than the bouillon paste.

## Goulash Soup

¼ cup olive oil
¼ lb. turkey bacon, diced
1 lb. beef or venison, cubed
2 medium onions, diced
1 leek (white part only), diced
1 green pepper, diced
1 sweet red pepper, diced
6 large cloves garlic, minced
3 medium tomatoes, peeled & diced
4 cups beef stock
3 Tbsp. paprika (yes, 3 Tbsp.)
1 Tbsp. caraway seeds
2 Tbsp. tomato paste
2 tsp. dried leaf thyme
2 tsp. dried leaf marjoram
1 tsp. salt
1 tsp. black pepper
2 15-oz. cans cannellini beans, rinsed & drained

Cut meat into ½" cubes and dice bacon and all vegetables before starting soup.  Pour oil into a 5 quart Dutch oven over medium-high heat.  Fry bacon until crisp.  Remove bacon with a slotted spoon and set aside.  Brown meat cubes in bacon drippings, stirring constantly, until cubes are browned on all sides.  Remove meat and set aside.  Sauté onions in drippings (add oil if needed) for 10-15 minutes, until browned.  Add meat, bacon, and remaining ingredients, except beans.  Stir well.  Bring mixture to a boil, reduce heat, and let simmer, uncovered, for 20 minutes, stirring occasionally.  Add beans and continue cooking another 15 minutes, until beans are heated through.  Serves 8.

Note:  beef stew meat, chuck roast, arm roast, venison steak, etc. will all work well.  Beef stock can be made with 4 cups water and 4 tsp.beef bouillon paste or 4 cubes beef bouillon.  Reduce salt if using beef boullion cubes versus the bouillon paste.

## Buffalo Stew

1 lb. ground beef or turkey
1 4-oz. can chopped mild green chilies
1 large onion, chopped
1 14.5-oz. can diced tomatoes
1 15-oz. can ranch style
    or Mexican style chili beans
2 10.5-oz. cans beef consommé, undiluted
1 14.5-oz. can peas & carrots, drained
1 14.5-oz can green beans, drained

Mix ground beef or turkey with green chilies.  Brown mixture and onions in a large non-stick skillet until liquid has evaporated.  Add remaining ingredients.  Place in a slow cooker and cook on low for 3 hours.  Serves 6-8. Variation:  for a spicier stew add another can of chili beans.

**84**

## Greek Chili

1 Tbsp. olive oil
2 large boneless, skinless chicken breasts
1 small red onion, chopped
2 cloves garlic, minced
4 tsp. chili powder
1 tsp. dried oregano
¼ tsp. black pepper
1 14.5-oz. can diced tomatoes, undrained
1 quart spaghetti sauce
1 16-oz. can pinto beans, rinsed & drained
⅓ cup chopped green pepper
1 cup diced zucchini

### Topping

⅓-½ cup crumbled feta cheese

Cut chicken breasts into 1 inch cubes. Heat oil in a heavy soup pot and add chicken. Cook and stir until chicken is lightly browned, about 4 minutes. Add onions and continue to cook for 3 more minutes or until onions begin to soften. Add remaining ingredients, except green pepper and zucchini. Bring to a boil. Reduce heat to simmer. Add green pepper and zucchini. Cover and simmer for 15 minutes. Remove from heat. Ladle chili into bowls and top with feta cheese. Serves 5.

## Jamaican Stew

1 medium onion, chopped
1 green pepper, chopped
2 ½ cups cauliflower florets,
    chopped to bite-size
2 cups small, unpeeled, diced zucchini
4 cloves garlic, minced
1 15.5-oz. package frozen cut green beans
½ cup tomato paste
1 14.5-oz. can crushed tomatoes, undrained
1 15.5-oz. can garbanzo beans,
    rinsed & drained
2 cups water
2 tsp. vegetable bouillon paste or 2 cubes vegetable bouillon*
1½ tsp. paprika
1 tsp. salt
¾ tsp. allspice

Combine all ingredients in a Dutch oven. Bring to a boil. Reduce heat to a simmer. Cover and simmer for 20-25 minutes, until vegetables are tender. Stir often. Stew may appear to have too little liquid, but vegetables will give up juice while cooking. Serves 8-10.

*Better than Bouillon™ is the bouillon paste recommended. If using bouillon cubes reduce or eliminate the salt as bouillon cubes contain more salt than the bouillon paste.

## Savory Italian Sausage & Kidney Bean Soup

1-1¼ lbs. Italian seasoned ground turkey
1 medium onion, diced
2 Tbsp. olive oil
3 cups water
3 tsp. chicken bouillon paste or 3 cubes chicken
    bouillon*
3 cups jicama, diced small
1 14.5-oz. can crushed
    or stewed tomatoes, undrained
2 Tbsp. apple cider vinegar
½ cup chopped green pepper
½ tsp. Vege-Sal® or seasoning salt
½ tsp. dry ground mustard
¼ tsp. sage
¼ tsp. chili powder
½ tsp. fresh ground pepper
1 16-oz. can dark red kidney beans, rinsed & drained

In a large, heavy soup pot cook sausage and onion in olive oil until lightly browned. Add remaining ingredients except for kidney beans. Bring to a boil. Reduce heat, cover and simmer for 1½ hours. Add beans and heat through. Jicama will stay tender-crisp. Makes about 2 quarts and serves 8.

*Better than Bouillon™ is the bouillon paste recommended. If using bouillon cubes reduce or eliminate the salt as bouillon cubes contain more salt than the bouillon paste.

## Quick & Spicy Taco Soup

1 large onion, chopped
1 lb. ground beef or turkey
1 15-oz. can tomato sauce
1 14.5-oz. can diced tomatoes
    with green chilies
1 10-oz. can enchilada sauce
1 10.75-oz. can tomato soup, undiluted
1 15-oz. can pinto beans, rinsed & drained
1 15-oz. can red kidney beans,
    rinsed & drained
1 15-oz. can black beans, rinsed & drained
4 cups water
1 tsp. salt
1 packet taco seasoning

### Toppings:
Sour cream
Shredded cheddar cheese

In a Dutch oven, brown ground beef with onion. Drain. Add remaining ingredients, except topping. Bring to a boil. Reduce heat and simmer for 1 hour, stirring occasionally. Ladle into bowls and top with sour cream and cheese. Serves 8.

## Southwestern Bean Soup

2 Tbsp. extra virgin olive oil
1 yellow sweet pepper, diced
1 large sweet onion, chopped
4 cloves garlic, minced
2 14-oz. cans black beans,
    rinsed & drained
1 19-oz. can cannellini beans,
    rinsed & drained
1 15-oz. can dark red kidney beans,
    rinsed & drained
1 14.5-oz. can diced tomatoes
    w/sweet onions
1 14.5-oz. can diced tomatoes
    w/roasted garlic
1 4-oz. can chopped black olives
1 4-oz. can diced green chilies
1½ tsp. chili powder
1½ Tbsp. beef bouillon paste or 4 cubes beef bouillon*
1 quart water

Heat olive oil in a soup pot or Dutch oven. Sauté onion and garlic until translucent, about 5 minutes. Add yellow peppers and sauté until tender-crisp. Add beans to onion mixture in pot. Add remaining ingredients and bring to boil. Reduce heat and simmer for 10 minutes. Serves 10-12.
Variation for slow cooker: Mix together soup as above, omitting yellow peppers. Do not bring to a boil, but pour into a slow cooker. Cook on low for 4 hours. Sauté yellow peppers separately and add just before serving.

*Better than Bouillon™ is the bouillon paste recommended. If using bouillon cubes soup will be saltier.

## Southern-Style Stew

4 parsnips, peeled & sliced
1 15-oz. can black-eyed peas,
    rinsed & drained
1-2 15-oz. cans cut green beans,
    drained
1 medium onion, chopped
1 lb. small beef smoked sausages
    (such as Lil' Smokies™)
½ cup beef broth
2 Tbsp. butter

In a 4 quart slow cooker, layer ingredients in order given. Dot with butter. Cook on low for 4-5 hours, until parsnips are tender but not mushy. Serves 10.

**87**

## Bean and Sausage Stew

2 Tbsp. olive oil
1 14-oz. ring beef or turkey kielbasa,
    sliced
2 cloves garlic, thinly sliced
2 16-oz. cans navy beans,
    rinsed & drained
1 14.5-oz. can diced tomatoes, undrained
1-1¾ cups water
2 tsp. chicken bouillon paste or 2 cubes chicken
    bouillon*
¼ tsp. black pepper
1 tsp. Italian seasoning, chili powder,
    or curry powder (optional)
1 bunch kale, de-ribbed and chopped

Heat oil in a soup pot over medium heat. Add sausage cubes and brown on all sides. Reduce heat and add garlic. Cook garlic for about 2 minutes. Add beans, water, bouillon, tomatoes, pepper, and one of the seasonings listed (if desired). Stir, scraping bottom of pan. Bring to a boil, then reduce heat to simmer. To de-rib kale, fold each kale leaf in half lengthwise and remove stem by ripping or cutting it out. Add kale to stew and stir until kale is wilted, about 2 minutes. For a mellow stew, leave out optional seasonings. Serves 4-5.

*Better than Bouillon™ is the bouillon paste recommended. If using bouillon cubes stew will be saltier.

## Fried Kielbasa Soup

1 Tbsp. butter
1 Tbsp. olive oil
1 16-oz. ring beef kielbasa, sliced
1 large onion, chopped
6 stalks celery, chopped
1 lb. bag frozen sliced carrots, thawed
3 cups water
2 11.5-oz. cans bean with bacon soup,
    undiluted
1 16-oz. can navy beans, rinsed & drained

In a Dutch oven, heat butter and oil. Add a single layer of sliced kielbasa. Fry on both sides until brown. Remove kielbasa with a slotted spoon. Repeat until all kielbasa is fried. Set aside. Sauté onion, celery, and carrots in drippings until tender. Add remaining ingredients, including kielbasa slices. Stir well and heat until piping hot. Serves 8.

## Baked Bean & Chicken Stew

2 Tbsp. olive oil
1 cup chopped onion
1 medium green pepper, chopped
1 large clove garlic, minced
¾ lb. boneless, skinless chicken breast,
    cut into ½" cubes
2 16-oz. cans baked beans,
    rinsed & drained
1 8-oz. can baked beans,
    rinsed, drained, & pureed
½ cup chicken broth
1 15-oz. can garbanzo beans,
    rinsed & drained
1 14.5-oz. can diced tomatoes, undrained
¾ tsp. rubbed sage
½ tsp. ground cumin

In a Dutch oven over medium heat, sauté onion, green pepper, and garlic in oil until tender. Add chicken and stir until chicken is done, 5-8 minutes. Puree the 8-oz. can of beans with the chicken broth. Add to chicken mixture. Stir in remaining ingredients. Simmer uncovered 15-20 minutes. Serves 6-8.
Variation: replace chicken with 1-2 12.5-oz. cans chunk chicken breast, drained. Add with beans and tomatoes.

## Kickin' Chicken Taco Stew

1 stalk celery, diced
1 small to medium zucchini,
    peeled & diced
1 medium onion, chopped
1 16-oz. can black beans, undrained
1 16-oz. can kidney beans. undrained
1 8-oz. can tomato sauce
2 14.5-oz. cans diced tomatoes
    with chilies
1 packet (⅓ cup) taco seasoning
3 large boneless, skinless chicken breasts
**Toppings:**
Sour cream
Shredded cheddar cheese

Mix all ingredients, except chicken, in slow cooker. Lay the chicken breasts on top of stew. Cover and cook on low for 6 hours. Remove chicken and shred. Place back into stew and stir. Serve with toppings. Variations: for less heat, replace one or both cans of tomatoes with chilies with plain diced tomatoes. Serves 10-14.

## Quick Kids' Stew

12 oz. all beef ring sausage, ring bologna,
or any fully cooked sausage, sliced
1 Tbsp. butter
1 10.75-oz. can tomato soup, undiluted
1 11.25-oz. can bean with bacon soup,
    undiluted
½ soup can water
½ cup Almond Milk (page 107)
1 cup baked beans, rinsed & drained
2 cups frozen baby bean & carrot blend,
    thawed and sliced in ⅓'s
1 tsp. dried onion flakes
¼ tsp. black pepper

Heat butter in a large non-stick skillet. Brown sliced bologna or sausage on both sides. Add remaining ingredients. Simmer until hot and vegetables are tender-crisp. Serves 8.

## Cheesy Kielbasa Soup

2 Tbsp. butter
1 lb. kielbasa sausage
1 cup chopped onion
1 cup chopped celery
4 large carrots, peeled & diced
2 cloves garlic, minced
9½ cups water
2 Tbsp. chicken bouillon paste or 6 cubes
    chicken bouillon*
1 lb. dry lentils, sorted & rinsed
½ tsp. black pepper
½ tsp. basil
1 small bay leaf
½ cup shredded cheddar cheese

Slice kielbasa ¼" thick. Heat butter in a large non-stick skillet. Fry slices until very brown on both sides. Fry in batches and set aside. Sauté onion, celery, carrots, and garlic in drippings (add 1 Tbsp. butter if needed) until tender-crisp, 5-10 minutes. Add 2 cups of water. Stir well to get all the drippings from the pan. Pour into a soup pot. Add remaining water, chicken bouillon, lentils, pepper, basil, and bay leaf. Bring to a boil. Reduce heat and simmer 45 minutes. Remove bay leaf and stir in shredded cheddar cheese and kielbasa slices. Heat through. This soup is thick, almost a stew. Serves 6-8.

*Better than Bouillon™ is the bouillon paste recommended. If using bouillon cubes soup will be saltier.

## Mindless Meatball Soup

1 14.5-oz can stewed tomatoes
1 14.5-oz. can chicken broth
1 14.5-oz. can beef broth
1 15-oz. can red kidney beans,
    rinsed & drained
16-oz. frozen vegetables, your choice
18-oz. frozen Italian meatballs
1½ tsp. Italian seasoning

### Topping:
6 Tbsp. grated Parmesan cheese

In a large Dutch oven or soup pot, mix all ingredients except cheese. Bring to a boil. Reduce heat and simmer 15-20 minutes, until vegetables and meatballs are hot. Ladle into bowls and top each bowl with 1 Tbsp. Parmesan cheese. Serve immediately. Serves 6.

## Meatball Stew

### Meatballs:
1 lb. ground beef
1 egg
¼ cup oat bran
1 heaping tsp. onion flakes
½ tsp. salt
### Stew:
2 Tbsp. olive oil (for frying)
1 10.75-oz. can tomato soup, condensed
1 soup can water
2 tsp. beef bouillon paste or 2 cubes beef
    bouillon*
¼ tsp. thyme
1 14.5-oz. can sliced carrots, drained
1 15.5-oz. can black beans, rinsed & drained
1 8-oz. can small whole onions, drained
1 cup frozen green beans

Mix meatball ingredients in a bowl. Shape into about 34 meatballs, using a small trigger-style scoop or a rounded teaspoonful of meat per ball. In a heavy pan or Dutch oven, brown meatballs in heated olive oil. Add remaining stew ingredients and stir well. Cook over low heat 15-20 minutes, stirring occasionally. Serves 6-8.

Variation: replace ½ cup frozen pearl onions with canned onions.

*Better than Bouillon™ is the bouillon paste recommended. If using bouillon cubes reduce or eliminate the salt as bouillon cubes contain more salt than the bouillon paste.

## Navy Bean and Turkey Bacon Soup

6 slices of turkey bacon
1-2 Tbsp. olive oil
1 cup chopped onion
1 cup chopped celery
1 cup chopped carrots
2 cloves garlic, minced
4 cups chicken broth, divided
1 tsp. thyme
¾ tsp. marjoram
2 16-oz. cans navy beans, drained & rinsed
2 bay leaves
¼ tsp. salt
½ tsp. black pepper

In a large soup pot over medium heat, cook bacon in oil until crisp. Stir often so it does not burn. Stir in onions, celery, carrots, garlic and ½ cup of chicken broth. Cook and stir for 5 minutes until vegetables are tender-crisp. Add thyme and marjoram and cook 1 minute more. Add remaining chicken broth, beans, bay leaves, salt, and pepper. Bring just to a boil then reduce heat. Cover and simmer for 30 minutes. Remove bay leaves. Carefully ladle half of the soup into a blender. Puree until smooth then pour back into soup pot and mix well. Serves 6.

Variation: replace chicken broth with 4 cups water and 4 tsp. chicken bouillon paste or 4 cubes chicken bouillon.*
*Better than Bouillon™ is the bouillon paste recommended. If using bouillon cubes eliminate the salt as bouillon cubes contain more salt than the bouillon paste.

## Creamy Lima Bean Soup

1 Tbsp. olive oil
1 small onion, diced
1 large clove garlic, minced
2 cups water
2 tsp. vegetable bouillon paste or 2 cubes
    vegetable bouillon*
2 cups frozen lima beans
½ tsp. salt (or to taste)
¼ tsp. black pepper

In a Dutch oven heat oil over medium heat. Add onion and garlic and cook until tender. Add remaining ingredients and bring to a boil. Reduce heat immediately and simmer 10-15 minutes or until beans are tender. Pour soup into food processor or blender and puree until smooth. Return soup to pan and heat again if needed. Garnish with chives and serve. Serves 4-5.
Variation: replace water and bouillon with 2 cups vegetable broth.
*Better than Bouillon™ is the bouillon paste recommended. If using bouillon cubes reduce or eliminate the salt as bouillon cubes contain more salt than the bouillon paste.

## Curried Limas & Parsnip Soup

1½ cups dried lima beans
8 cups water, divided
1 lb. parsnips, peeled & diced
2 carrots, diced
1½ tsp. salt
1 16-oz. container sour cream
1 tsp. curry powder
1 tsp. black pepper

Soak beans overnight in 6 cups water.  Rinse and drain.  Place beans and 2 cups water into a 3-4 quart slow cooker.  Cook on high for 4-5 hours, until beans are beginning to get tender.  Add parsnips, carrots, and salt.  Continue cooking on high for 1 hour, or until parsnips and carrots are tender.  Add sour cream, curry powder, and pepper.  Cook 10 minutes longer.  Add more curry if desired.  Serves 8.

## Manhattan Cod Chowder

3 Tbsp. butter
2 large onions, chopped
1 large yellow or orange sweet pepper, chopped
1 cup chopped celery
2 cloves garlic, minced
2 large carrots, diced
2 14-oz. cans diced tomatoes, undrained
1 16-oz. can navy or kidney beans,
    rinsed & drained
1½ tsp. salt
2 lbs. cod or white fish of your choice

### Almond Cream:
1 cup raw almonds
2 cups water
Cheesecloth

Melt butter in a Dutch oven.  Sauté onions, yellow pepper, celery, garlic, and carrots over medium heat for 5 minutes.  Add tomatoes, beans and salt.  Cover and simmer for 10 minutes, or until vegetables are tender-crisp.  Chowder will be very thick.  Stir often.  Meanwhile, place almonds into a blender and blend until crumbly.  Add water and blend for several minutes to liquefy almonds.  Place a colander into a bowl.  Fold several layers of cheesecloth and place into colander.  Slowly pour almond cream into cheesecloth.  Lift up edges of cheesecloth and twist to extract cream.  Discard almond meal and cheesecloth when done, or set aside for another use.  Cut fish into 1" pieces.  Add fish and almond cream to chowder.  Simmer for 15 minutes.  This soup is best made ahead of time (at least an hour or two) to let the flavors blend.  Reheat to serve.  Serves 6-8.

**93**

## Hearty Bean Soup

2 Tbsp. butter
1 large onion, chopped
1 medium green pepper, chopped
2 cloves garlic, minced
2 15-oz. cans navy beans, rinsed & drained
2 15-oz. cans pinto beans, rinsed & drained
2 11.5-oz. cans bean with bacon soup,
    undiluted
2 cups diced turkey ham
2 cups water
3 Tbsp. chipotle salsa (drained or thick)

In a Dutch oven, heat butter.  Sauté onions and green peppers for about 3 minutes.  Add garlic and cook 1 minute longer.  Add remaining ingredients.  Cover and cook over medium to medium-low heat for 20 minutes, stirring occasionally.  Cook until hot. Serves 10.

## Cheesy Bean & Broccoli Soup

2 16-oz. cans navy beans, rinsed & drained
2 cups water
2 tsp. vegetable bouillon paste or 2 cubes
vegetable bouillon*
1 lb. frozen chopped broccoli, thawed
8 oz. cheddar cheese, shredded
1 10.75-oz. can cream of celery soup,
    undiluted
¼ tsp. black pepper

Place 1 can navy beans, bouillon, and a little of the water called for into a food processor.  Puree until smooth.  Pour into a 3-4 quart slow cooker and add remaining ingredients.  Cook on low for 3 hours.

*Better than Bouillon™ is the bouillon paste recommended.  If using bouillon cubes soup will be saltier.

## Roasted Vegetable Soup

1 medium eggplant, cut into ¾" pieces
2 medium zucchini, cut into ¾" pieces
2 large sweet red peppers, cut into ¾" pieces
4 parsnips, peeled and cut into ¾" pieces
2 large carrots, peeled and diced
1 medium leek, white part only,
    washed & sliced
3 Tbsp. extra virgin olive oil, divided
6 cloves garlic, minced
1¾ quarts water
3 Tbsp. bouillon paste or 6 cubes bouillon, beef
    or chicken*
1 16-oz. can kidney beans, rinsed & drained
1 15.5-oz. can garbanzo beans, rinsed & drained
1 15-oz. can black-eyed peas, rinsed & drained
1 Tbsp. apple cider vinegar
1 tsp. dried rosemary, crushed
1 tsp. dried marjoram
½ tsp. rubbed sage
½ tsp. thyme

Line two 10x15" pans with foil. Spray foil with oil and spread eggplant, zucchini, red peppers, parsnips, carrots, and leeks evenly into pans. Pour 1 Tbsp. oil over each pan of vegetables and coat by mixing with hands. Roast vegetables, uncovered, at 425° for 30 minutes. If staggering pans, switch pans on oven racks every 10 minutes. Stir vegetables every 10 minutes. Heat remaining 1 Tbsp. olive oil in a Dutch oven or soup pot. Sauté garlic in hot oil for 2 minutes, stirring constantly. Add roasted vegetables and remaining ingredients. Bring to a boil, reduce heat and simmer for 5-10 minutes. Makes 4 quarts.

*Better than Bouillon™ is the bouillon paste recommended. If using bouillon cubes soup will be saltier.

## Santa Fe Cheese Soup

2 cups water
2 tsp. chicken bouillon paste or 2 cubes chicken
    bouillon*
2 15-oz. cans black beans,
    rinsed & drained
1 14.5-oz. can diced tomatoes, undrained
1 4-oz. can chopped green chilies
1 10-oz. can premium chunk white chicken,
    drained
8 oz. cheddar cheese, shredded

In a 3 quart saucepan, combine water and bouillon. Add remaining ingredients. Cook, stirring gently until cheese has melted. Soup is best made ahead of time and reheated. Makes about 2 quarts and serves 6.

*Better than Bouillon™ is the bouillon paste recommended. If using bouillon cubes soup will be saltier.

## Northern Tomato Soup

1 Tbsp. olive oil
1 large sweet onion, diced
2 stalks celery, diced
2 cloves garlic, minced
2 14-oz. cans or 1 28-oz. can
    crushed tomatoes
2 10.75-oz. cans tomato soup, undiluted
4 cups water
1½ Tbsp. vegetable bouillon paste or 4 cubes vegetable
    bouillon*
2 15.5-oz. cans great northern beans,
    rinsed & drained
1 Tbsp. tomato paste
1½ tsp. basil
1 tsp. oregano
1 tsp. thyme
¼-½ tsp. salt, opt.

Heat oil in a Dutch oven or soup pot. Sauté onions, garlic, and celery until tender. Add remaining ingredients, except salt, and mix well. Bring to a boil, reduce heat and simmer for 10 minutes. Taste soup and add salt if needed. If a thicker soup is desired, puree 1 can of the beans with a little soup broth before adding. Serves 8-10.

*Better than Bouillon™ is the bouillon paste recommended. If using bouillon cubes reduce or eliminate the salt as bouillon cubes contain more salt than the bouillon paste.

# Main Dishes

## Bacon & Egg Breakfast Burrito

### Burrito:
1 Tbsp. butter
1 egg, beaten
2 slices turkey bacon, diced
    & fried crisp
Salt to taste
Black pepper to taste

### Filling:
¼ cup Delicious Refried Beans (page150)
2 Tbsp. shredded cheddar cheese

### Toppings:
1 Tbsp. salsa
1 Tbsp. sour cream

Heat butter in a small non-stick skillet. Pour in beaten egg all at once. Swirl pan gently so egg completely covers the bottom of pan. Immediately sprinkle on bacon, salt, and pepper. Cook for 1-2 minutes. Carefully flip with a spatula and cook other side 1-2 minutes. Heat refried beans in separate pan or in microwave while egg is cooking. Slide egg burrito onto a plate. Spread hot refried beans over top of burrito and sprinkle with cheese. Roll up as you would a crepe. Spread salsa and sour cream along the top. Serves 1.

Variations:   replace bacon with browned turkey sausage, fried diced turkey ham, or sautéed diced green peppers and onions.

## Cheesy Egg Puffs

10 eggs
1 tsp. baking powder
½ cup garbanzo bean flour
½ cup butter, softened
1 small can mushrooms, drained & chopped
½ small onion, chopped
4 cups shredded Monterey Jack cheese
2 cups small curd cottage cheese

Beat eggs in large bowl. Blend ingredients into eggs one at a time. Fill oil-sprayed muffin tins. Bake at 350º for 40 minutes. Makes 2 dozen puffs. Reheat in microwave.

## Breakfast Casserole

1 lb. ground turkey breakfast sausage
2 large green or red sweet peppers, chopped
1 large onion, chopped
3 Roma tomatoes, diced
3 16-oz. cans pinto beans, rinsed & drained
½ tsp. salt
1 dozen eggs
2 cups shredded cheddar cheese

Brown sausage in a large non-stick skillet, breaking it into small chunks as it cooks. Use a little oil if necessary. Add peppers and onion. Cook until vegetables are tender-crisp. Add beans and salt. Continue cooking until beans are hot. Stir in tomatoes. Pour into an oil-sprayed 9x13" casserole dish. Beat eggs and pour evenly over bean mixture. Sprinkle cheese on top. Cover with foil. Bake at 350° for 45-50 minutes. Casserole should be bubbling and steamy. Remove from oven, remove foil, and allow to sit 10-15 minutes before serving. Serves 8.

Variation: replace sausage with turkey bacon or turkey ham. Dice meat and fry in a little oil until bacon is crisp or ham is browned before adding.

## Spanish Eggs

1 Tbsp. butter
1 Tbsp. finely chopped onion
1 Tbsp. finely chopped green pepper
2 eggs
2 Tbsp. pinto beans or baked beans,
  rinsed & drained
2-4 Tbsp. shredded cheddar cheese
3-4 Tbsp. salsa, warmed
Whole lettuce leaves or shredded lettuce

Heat butter in a saucepan. Sauté onion and green pepper until tender-crisp. Add eggs and scramble until soft set. Add beans and continue to scramble until done. Sprinkle cheese on egg mixture and cover pan until cheese melts (on low or with heat turned off). Spread with salsa. Serve rolled like a burrito in lettuce leaves or on top of shredded lettuce or in a **Chickpea Tortilla (page 175)**. Serves one.

Variation: replace beans with refried beans, mixing beans into eggs after eggs are cooked and before adding cheese.

## Huevos Rancheros

1 15-oz. can black beans,
   rinsed & drained
1¾ cups salsa
¼ cup water
4 large eggs
Salt and black pepper
4 Tbsp. shredded cheddar cheese
   or Mexican cheese blend

Mix together black beans, salsa, and water in a 10" skillet. Heat to boiling over high heat, stirring frequently. Break eggs one at a time into a custard cup. Slip each egg into skillet on top of boiling bean mixture. Salt and pepper to taste. Reduce heat to medium-low. Cover and simmer 5-7 minutes or until whites are completely set and yolks begin to thicken, or until eggs are cooked to desired taste. Turn off heat. Sprinkle eggs with shredded cheese and cover until cheese starts to melt. Serve immediately. Serves 3-4.

## Sausage Gravy and Bean Casserole

4 15-oz. cans navy beans, rinsed & drained
1 lb. ground turkey sausage

### Chicken Gravy:
⅔ cup water
2 cups Almond Milk (page 107)
4 tsp. chicken bouillon paste or 4 cubes chicken
   bouillon*
¼ cup+2 Tbsp. garbanzo bean flour
Salt and black pepper to taste, optional

### Topping:
1 cup shredded Monterey Jack
   or cheddar cheese

Spray a 9x13" casserole dish with oil. In a frying pan cook the sausage. Pour beans and sausage into casserole dish. In a small sauce pan, combine all gravy ingredients, except salt and pepper. Whisk until smooth and free of lumps. Heat to boiling, stirring constantly. When bubbly and thick, let cook for 1 minute longer. Stir into bean mixture. Taste before adding salt and pepper. Bake uncovered at 350º for 30-45 minutes, or until hot and bubbly all over. Top with cheese if desired. Bake for 5 minutes longer, or just until cheese has melted. Allow to set 5-10 minutes to absorb liquid. Serves 6.

*Better than Bouillon™ is the bouillon paste recommended. If using bouillon cubes reduce or eliminate the salt as bouillon cubes contain more salt than the bouillon paste.

## Chicken Lentil Divan

2 boneless skinless chicken breasts
2 Tbsp. butter
1 10.5-oz. can cream of chicken soup,
    undiluted
⅓ cup Almond Milk (page 107)
¼-½ tsp. salt, to taste
1 16-oz. bag frozen green beans, broccoli,
    or frozen vegetable blend of choice, thawed
¾ cup cooked lentils
½ cup shredded cheddar cheese

Slice chicken breasts in half crosswise to make 4 chicken breast pieces. Melt butter in a large non-stick skillet or Dutch oven. Add chicken breasts and brown well on both sides. Remove chicken and set aside. Add soup and milk to drippings in skillet and stir. Pour half of soup mixture into a bowl and set aside. Add salt, green beans, and lentils to other half of soup mixture in skillet. Mix well. Pour green bean mixture into a casserole dish and top with chicken pieces. Spoon reserved soup over chicken breasts. Bake uncovered at 400° for 45 minutes. Sprinkle with cheese and bake 5 minutes longer. Let sit for 5 minutes before serving. Serves 5-6.

## Peppery Chicken Stir Fry

2 Tbsp. olive oil
1 large carrot, diced
1 large onion, chopped
1 sweet red pepper, chopped
1 cup chopped broccoli
1 small yellow zucchini squash, diced
4-5 cloves garlic, minced
1 tsp. basil
1 tsp. oregano
1 tsp. black pepper
½ tsp. dried leaf thyme
2 Tbsp. soy liquid aminos or soy sauce
1 15.5-oz. can garbanzo beans
    or cannellini beans, rinsed & drained
1 12.5-oz. can chunk white chicken breast, drained

Heat oil in a large non-stick skillet or wok. Add carrots and stir fry for 3 minutes. Add remaining ingredients, except beans and chicken. Stir fry vegetables until tender-crisp. Add beans and chicken. Stir fry until heated through. Serves 6.

## Chicken Fajitas

1 lb. boneless, skinless chicken breast
1 15-oz. can red kidney beans,
   rinsed & drained
1 14.5-oz. can diced tomatoes, drained
1 4-oz. can diced green chilies
1 medium green pepper, julienned
1 medium yellow pepper, julienned
1 medium sweet red pepper, julienned
1 medium onion, halved & sliced
1 packet fajita seasoning
2 tsp. chili powder
2 tsp. garlic powder
Chickpea Tortillas (page 175)

### Toppings:
Shredded lettuce
Sour cream
Diced tomatoes

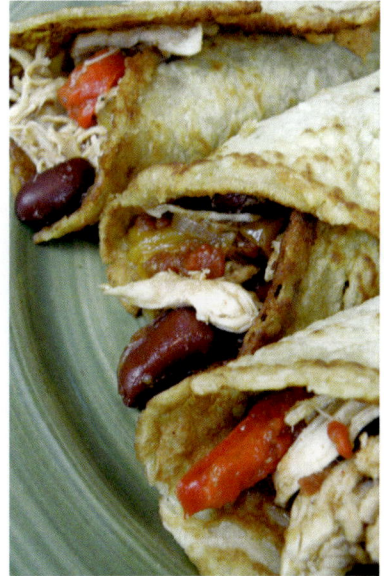

In a 3 quart slow cooker, mix together kidney beans, tomatoes, green chilies, peppers, onion, fajita mix, and spices. Slightly bury chicken breasts into vegetables. Cover and cook on low for 5-6 hours, or until chicken is tender. Remove chicken and shred with two forks. Return chicken to slow cooker and fold in. With a fork or slotted spoon spread fajita mixture down the center of each **Chickpea Tortilla**. Top with desired toppings. Juice may be drained from fajita mixture after replacing shredded chicken, if desired. Serves 6-8.

## Southern Lentil and Chicken Casserole

4 slices turkey bacon, diced
2 Tbsp. olive oil
2 Tbsp. butter
2 large carrots, chopped
1 medium onion, chopped
1 cup dried lentils , sorted & rinsed
1 15-oz. can black-eyed peas,
    rinsed & drained
1 14.5-oz. can Italian stewed tomatoes,
    undrained
1¾ cups water
1-2 tsp. chicken bouillon paste or 1-2 cubes
    chicken bouillon (to taste)*
2 Tbsp. sundried tomato pesto
2 cups ½" cubes cooked chicken or turkey

In a large non-stick skillet, fry bacon until crisp.  Remove bacon from pan and set aside.  Add butter, carrots, and onion to pan.  Cook over medium heat for 3-5 minutes, until vegetables are tender-crisp.  Stir in lentils and cook 3 minutes longer, stirring occasionally.  Add remaining ingredients, including bacon.  Mix well.  Pour into an oil-sprayed 9x13" casserole dish.  Cover with foil and bake at 350° for 1 hour and 15 minutes to 1 hour and 35 minutes, or until liquid is mostly absorbed and lentils are tender.  Leftover chicken or turkey works great with this dish.  Serves 6-8.

*Better than Bouillon™ is the bouillon paste recommended.  If using bouillon cubes casserole will be saltier.

# Chicken 'n' Biscuits

### Cheese Biscuits:
1 ½ cups garbanzo bean flour, sifted
½ cup oat bran
4 tsp. baking powder
1 tsp. cream of tartar
¼ tsp. salt
2 tsp. onion powder
2 Tbsp. safflower oil
½ cup water
2 cups cheddar cheese, diced or crumbled

### Chicken Filling:
2 stalks celery, diced
3 medium carrots, peeled & diced
1 medium onion, chopped
3 Tbsp. butter
¼ cup garbanzo bean flour
2 tsp. chicken bouillon paste or 2 cubes chicken bouillon*
1 cup Almond Milk (page 107)
1 cup water
1 10.75-oz. can cream of chicken soup
4 large chicken breasts
   or 4 cups cubed, cooked chicken

### Garnish:
**Paprika**

Boil chicken breasts for 25 minutes. Drain, allow to cool, and cut into 1" cubes. Combine biscuit ingredients. Work dough with hands to form a ball. Set aside. In a Dutch oven, sauté celery, carrots, and onion in butter until tender. Stir in flour and bouillon until blended. Gradually add the almond milk and water. Bring to a boil. Cook and stir for 2 minutes, until thickened. Stir in soup and chicken. Cook until hot and bubbly. Pour into an oil-sprayed 9x13" casserole dish. Divide biscuit dough into 12 portions. Shape into round biscuits (diameter approximately 2") ⅓-½" thick. Top chicken filling with the 12 biscuits. Garnish by sprinkling paprika over biscuits. Bake uncovered at 350º for 40 minutes, or until biscuits are lightly browned on top and bottom of biscuits are done. Lift biscuit with a fork to check bottom. Leftover chicken or turkey will work well in this recipe. Serves 6-8.

Note: Biscuits and filling can be made up ahead of time. When ready to cook, heat filling before placing biscuits on top. If filling is cold, biscuits will not get done on the bottom.

*Better than Bouillon™ is the bouillon paste recommended. If using bouillon cubes Chicken Filling will be saltier.

## Lima Chicken

1 chicken fryer, cut into pieces
   or 4-5 lbs. of chicken
2 Tbsp. butter
½ lb. baby carrots, sliced lengthwise
12 frozen pearl onions
1 10.75-oz. can cream of chicken soup
½ soup can of Almond Milk (page 107)
¼ tsp. sage
¼ tsp. salt
¼ tsp. black pepper
1 10-oz. package
   or 2 cups frozen baby lima beans

In a large non-stick skillet, brown chicken in melted butter. Remove chicken from pan and place into a sprayed 2 quart casserole dish. Set aside. Add carrots and onions to skillet and sauté in drippings for 2 minutes. Add soup, milk, sage, salt, and pepper. Stir well. Cover and cook over low heat for 10 minutes, stirring often. Add lima beans and stir well. Pour mixture over chicken. Cover and bake at 375° for 45 minutes. Uncover and bake an additional 15 minutes, or until chicken is tender. Serves 4-6.

## Italian Vegetable Bean Casserole

1 Tbsp. olive oil
1 4-oz. can sliced mushrooms,
   drained & chopped
½ cup chopped onion
½ cup chopped green pepper
½ cup chopped sweet red pepper
2½ cups cubed cooked chicken
1 15-oz. can black beans, rinsed & drained
1 cup frozen peas and carrots
1½ cups sour cream
1 cup shredded cheddar cheese
2 tsp. Italian seasoning
1 tsp. salt
½ tsp. black pepper

### Topping:
¾ cup shredded cheddar cheese

Heat oil in a large skillet. Add mushrooms, onions, and peppers. Sauté until onions and peppers are tender-crisp. Add remaining ingredients. Mix well and cook until hot. Transfer to an oil-sprayed 3 quart casserole dish. Bake uncovered at 350° for 30-35 minutes. Add cheese topping and bake a few minutes longer to melt cheese. Serves 8.

## Chicken & Chickpea à la King

4 cups cubed cabbage, optional
1 medium sweet onion, chopped
1 green pepper, seeded & chopped
3 Tbsp. butter
½ cup garbanzo or white bean flour
3 cups Almond Milk (recipe below)
1 Tbsp. soy liquid aminos or soy sauce
1 Tbsp. chopped fresh parsley
½ tsp. paprika
½ tsp. black pepper
3 Tbsp. chicken broth powder
1 4-oz. jar diced pimentos, drained
2 15-oz. cans garbanzo beans (chickpeas),
    rinsed & drained
1 10-oz. can premium chunk chicken, drained

Boil cabbage in a large pot for 30 minutes or until very limp. Drain and set aside. Sauté onion and green pepper in butter until tender. Add bean flour and stir until flour is smooth. Add almond milk and stir until smooth and mixture thickens. Add remaining ingredients and cabbage, if using. Cook over low heat 5-10 minutes, until all ingredients are hot. For saucier consistency, leave out cabbage.
Variation: leave out cabbage and serve over **Baking Powder Drop Biscuits (page 173).** Note: if purchasing almond milk, be sure to choose the unsweetened almond milk. Making your own almond milk is easy and less expensive than buying it. See recipe below.

## Almond Milk

1 cup raw almonds
4 cups water, divided
Note: Almond milk can be purchased at most grocery stores. Purchase the unsweetened non-vanilla flavored variety.

Soak almonds in 2 cups water for 3 hours or overnight in the refrigerator. Pour almonds and water into a blender and blend on high for 3 minutes.
Add as much of the remaining water as you can to the blended almonds and blend for 1 minute. Strain almond milk through several layers of cheese cloth, pressing to expel liquid.
Add any remaining water to the milk. Chill and use within a week.
Variation: for a no-soak method, blend almonds in blender until they become an even almond meal. Add water and blend for 3 minutes. Strain as above and chill. Makes about 4 cups. For almond cream use only 2 cups water.
Note: Can freeze in ¼-½ cup portions. The same can be done with store-bought almond milk. Measure milk into zipper-style freezer bags. Label and date bags.

## Texas Chow Mein

2 boneless, skinless chicken breasts
Salt and black pepper to taste
1 tsp. garlic powder
1 green pepper, chopped
1 sweet red pepper, chopped
1 16-oz. can cannellini beans,
    rinsed & drained
1 15-oz. can black beans,
    rinsed & drained
1 8-oz. jar (1 cup) chipotle salsa
Chicken flavored Cauli-rice (page 168)

### Toppings:
Shredded Mexican blend cheese
Sour cream

Cut chicken into cubes. Cook in small amount of oil until done. Drain if necessary. Add salt, pepper, garlic powder, green and red peppers. Sauté until peppers are tender-crisp. Add beans and salsa. Heat through. Serve over hot **Cauli-rice.** Serves 4.

Variation: for shredded chicken, cover and cook whole breasts in a little water until done. Remove and cool slightly. Shred with 2 forks. Add salt, pepper, and garlic powder to chicken. In a skillet, sauté green and red peppers in a little oil. Add chicken and remaining ingredients. Heat through. Serve over **Cauli-rice.** Top with cheese and sour cream.

## Cajun Black Beans & Ham

2 Tbsp. butter, divided
1½ cups cubed turkey ham
1 cup chopped onion
½ cup chopped sweet red pepper
1 15-oz. can black beans,
    rinsed & drained
¼ tsp. salt
½ tsp. Cajun seasoning
½ cup water, opt.

Melt 1 Tbsp. butter in a large non-stick skillet. Add ham and fry until browned, turning when necessary. Add remaining butter, onions, and red pepper to pan. Sauté until vegetables are tender-crisp. Add beans, salt, and pepper. Stir and heat through. For saucier beans add the water at the same time as the beans. Serve over chicken flavored **Cauli-rice (page 168)**, if desired. Serves 5-6.

## Pinto Turkey Ham

1 Tbsp. olive oil
1 medium onion, diced
15 baby carrots, diced
2-3 cups smoked turkey meat
1 16-oz. can pinto beans,
   rinsed & drained
1 cup water
1 tsp. Dijon mustard
½ tsp. purchased steak sauce
½ tsp. garlic powder
½-1 tsp. salt, to taste

Place 2-3 smoked turkey legs into a large soup pot and cover with water. Bring to a boil and simmer for 2 hours. Remove meat from bones and discard skin and bones. Strain broth and freeze for soup or other recipe. Heat oil in a large non-stick skillet. Sauté onions and carrots until tender-crisp. Add remaining ingredients, including turkey meat, and bring to a boil. Reduce heat to medium and continue to slowly boil for 10 minutes, or until liquid is reduced (by at least half) to a sauce. Stir occasionally. Serves 6.

Variation: use diced turkey ham instead of smoked turkey leg meat.

## Easy Pinto Beef Burritos

½-1 lb. beef round steak or venison steaks
Salt and black pepper to taste
3 cloves garlic, minced
1 15-oz. can pinto beans,
   rinsed & drained
1 4-oz. can diced green chilies
½ tsp. chili powder
Chickpea Tortillas (page 175)

### Toppings:
Salsa
Sour cream
Shredded cheddar cheese

Slice steak into thin strips, resembling fajita strips. Spray a large non-stick skillet with oil. Heat skillet over medium heat and add steak strips and garlic. Salt and pepper to taste. Cook until done, stirring occasionally to brown all sides. Stir in beans, green chilies, and chili powder. Cook until heated through. Serve in **Chickpea Tortillas**, topped with salsa, sour cream and cheese, or stuff into **Bacon and Egg Breakfast Burritos (page 99)**, replacing the bacon filling and adding cheese. Serves 4-6.

**109**

## Texicali Bean Bake

1 lb. ground beef
½ cup chopped onion
3 cloves garlic, minced
1 Tbsp. oil
2 sliced turkey bacon, diced
1 11.25-oz. can bean with bacon soup,
    undiluted
1 cup hot, spicy, or chipotle salsa
1 4-oz. can diced green chilies
1 15.5-oz. can black-eyed peas,
    rinsed & drained
1 15-oz. can black beans,
    rinsed & drained
2 cups shredded sharp cheddar cheese
½ tsp. salt
1 tsp. paprika
1 tsp. taco seasoning
½ tsp. black pepper

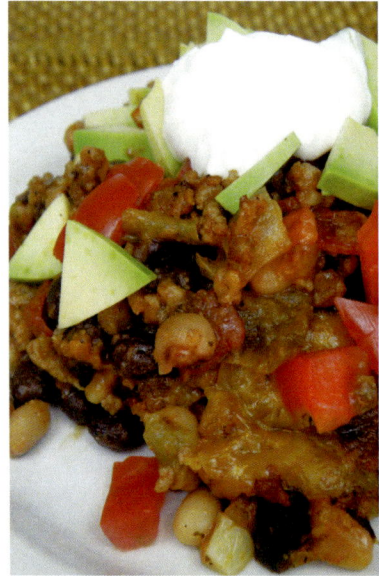

### Toppings:
Sour cream
Diced fresh tomatoes
Diced avocado

Brown ground beef, onion, and garlic in a large non-stick skillet. Drain and place into a large bowl. Pour oil in skillet and fry diced bacon until crisp. Remove with a slotted spoon and add to beef mixture. Add remaining ingredients, except ½ cup shredded cheese and toppings. Mix and pour into an oil-sprayed 9x13" casserole dish. Bake uncovered at 350º for 45 minutes, or until hot and bubbly. Sprinkle reserved cheese over top and cook 2-3 minutes longer. Let sit for 5-10 minutes before serving. Serve with toppings. Serves 8.

## Speedy Mexican Beef and Beans

1 lb. ground beef
1 packet taco seasoning
1 15-oz. can pinto or refried beans

Brown ground beef and drain well. Stir in seasoning mix and beans. Cook on low for 10-15 minutes. Serve with lettuce, cheese, salsa and sour cream. Makes 4-5 cups.

## Stuffed Mexican "Corn Bread"

### "Corn Bread":
½ cup garbanzo bean flour
½ cup oat bran
1½ tsp. baking powder
2 Tbsp. (½ packet) taco seasoning
3 Tbsp. oil
1 egg
1 cup salsa

### Layers:
2 cups shredded sharp cheddar cheese
1 medium onion, chopped
2 cloves garlic, minced
1 4-oz. can diced green chilies
1 lb. ground beef, cooked & drained
2 Tbsp. (½ packet) taco seasoning

Combine "corn bread" ingredients and mix well. Spray oil inside of 3½ quart slow cooker. Spread half of "corn bread" batter onto bottom of slow cooker. Layer cheese, onion, garlic, and green chilies on top of batter. Mix together cooked ground beef and taco seasoning. Spread beef mixture on top of green chilies layer. Dollop remaining "corn bread" batter on top of beef layer and gently spread out evenly to edges. Cook on low for 3-4 hours. Check bottom layer for doneness. Top will appear quite dark while cooking. Serves 6.

Variation: for larger slow cooker double recipe.

## Mexican Sundaes

### Cauli-rice:
1 16-oz. bag frozen cauliflower,
    thawed
¼ cup water
1-2 tsp. beef bouillon paste or 1-2 cubes beef bouillon*

### Meat mixture:
1 lb. lean ground beef
1 packet taco seasoning
½ cup water
4 cups cooked pinto, red,
    or kidney beans

### Toppings:
1 large yellow sweet pepper, diced
2 heads romaine lettuce,
    washed & shredded
6 Roma tomatoes, chopped
1 4.25-oz. can chopped black olives
1 cup shredded sharp cheddar cheese
1 cup salsa
1 cup sour cream
French or Western dressing

To make Cauli-rice, pulse in food processor until it resembles rice.  Place in pan with water and bouillon. Stir well.  Set aside.  In a skillet, brown and drain ground beef.  Add taco seasoning, water and beans.  Cook for 15 minutes.  Heat cauli-rice until just hot.  Build sundaes in the following order:  cauli-rice, beef mixture, yellow pepper, lettuce, tomatoes, olives, cheese, salsa, sour cream, and dressing.  Serves 8.
*Better than Bouillon™ is the bouillon paste recommended.  If using bouillon cubes recipe will be saltier.

## Quick Italian Beans

½ lb. ground beef
1 cup black beans or your favorite beans,
    rinsed & drained
½ cup spaghetti sauce
¼-½ cup shredded mozzarella cheese

Brown ground beef in a non-stick skillet and drain.
Add beans and spaghetti sauce and mix well.  Pour into a pie plate.  Sprinkle with cheese.  Place under broiler for a few moments until cheese melts.  Serves 4.

**112**

## Mexican Lentil Casserole

2 cups chopped cauliflower
1 medium sweet onion, diced
1 medium green pepper, diced
3 stalks celery, diced
2 Tbsp. olive oil
3½ cups water
1 cup dry green or brown lentils, rinsed
1 6-oz. can tomato paste
2 Tbsp. taco seasoning
½-1 tsp. chili powder, to taste
2 tsp. chicken bouillon paste or 2 cubes chicken bouillon*
**Topping:**
1½ cups shredded cheddar
   or Monterey Jack cheese

Place cauliflower into a food processor.  Pulse until cauliflower resembles rice, scraping down sides as needed.  Heat olive oil in a large non-stick skillet over medium heat.  Sauté cauliflower, onions, green peppers, and celery for 5 minutes.  Add water and bring to a boil.  Stir in lentils.  Cover, reduce heat, and simmer for 40 minutes.  Do not drain.  Add remaining ingredients, except cheese.  Pour into an oil-sprayed medium-sized casserole dish.  Bake uncovered at 350º for 20 minutes.  Sprinkle cheese on top and bake another 5 minutes, or until cheese melts.  Serves 8-10.
*Better than Bouillon™ is the bouillon paste recommended.  If using bouillon cubes recipe will be saltier.

## "Corn" Dogs

12. oz. beef franks (approximately 7)
7-10 wooden skewers (i.e. popsicle sticks)
**Batter:**
1 cup garbanzo bean flour
⅔ cup Almond Milk (page 107)
1 tsp. taco seasoning
1 tsp. xanthan gum (dough enhancer)
¾ tsp. baking powder
½ tsp. salt

Push sticks into franks.  Dry franks with paper towel.  Whisk batter ingredients together.  Dip franks into batter, completely covering with batter.  If batter is too thick, thin with 1-2 Tbsp. of water.  Drop corn dogs into preheated oil in deep fryer.  Fry about 2 minutes, until golden brown, turning when necessary.  Set onto paper towels when done.  If using a small fryer, cut franks in half before dipping in batter.
Variation:  use batter for deep-frying vegetables or cheese curds.  Cauliflower, green beans, broccoli, and onions all work well.  Leftover batter can also be used to make **Funnel Cakes.**  To make funnel cakes, drizzle batter from a spoon into hot oil, overlapping the drizzled lines several times.  End result will look like a snowflake. Fry until golden brown, and carefully remove. Fried batter can also be crumbled and used as a crispy salad topping.

## Chili Bread Olé

1 recipe Cheesy Chili Corn Bread (page 175)

**Meat Sauce:**
1 lb. ground beef
1 cup chopped onion
1 15-oz. can black beans, rinsed & drained
1 14-oz. can diced tomatoes, drained
1 8-oz. can tomato sauce
1½ tsp. chili powder
½ tsp. garlic powder
¼ tsp. oregano

**Toppings:**
Shredded cheddar cheese
Shredded lettuce
Chopped tomatoes
Sliced ripe olives
Sour cream
Salsa

In a large skillet or saucepan, brown ground beef and onion. Drain. Add remaining meat sauce ingredients. Bring to a boil. Reduce heat and simmer 15 minutes. Slice **Cheesy Chili Corn Bread** and place slices into a toaster, standing upright so they are easy to remove. Place toasted bread onto a plate and spoon meat sauce over top. Add any or all desired toppings. Serves 6.

## Kielbasa & Bean Sandwich Spread

½ lb. Kielbasa sausage, sliced
1 16-oz. can baked beans,
    rinsed & drained
2 Tbsp. ketchup
2 Tbsp. prepared yellow mustard

Place Kielbasa into a food processor and pulse to coarsely chop. Add remaining ingredients and pulse to blend and coarsely chop mixture. Heat and serve on **Bean Flour Yeast Bread (page 171)**, **Bruschetta (page 172)**, **Baking Powder Drop Biscuits (page 173)**, green pepper wedges, or stuff into hollowed out tomatoes. Top open face sandwiches with dill pickle slices. Serves 4.

**Variation:** replace Kielbasa with 1-1½ cups coarsely chopped bologna or salami. Makes 2 cups of spread.

## Italian Burger & Beans

1½ lbs. ground beef, browned & drained
1 medium onion, chopped
1 14.5-oz. can petite-cut diced tomatoes
     with garlic & olive oil
1-1½ tsp. Italian seasoning
2 15-oz. cans red kidney beans,
     rinsed & drained
1 cup beef broth

Place browned ground beef in bottom of an oil-sprayed 3 quart slow cooker.  Mix together remaining ingredients and pour over ground beef.  Cover and cook on low for 4-6 hours.  Serves 8.

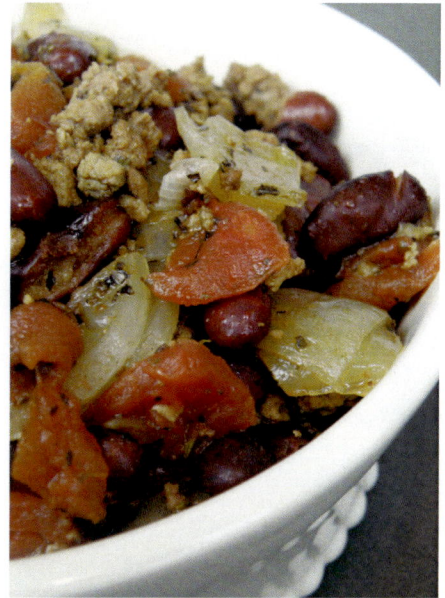

Variation:   replace beef broth with 1 cup of hot water and 1 tsp. beef bouillon paste or 1 cube beef bouillon.*

*Better than Bouillon™ is the bouillon paste recommended.  If using bouillon cubes recipe will be saltier.

## Italian Chuck Tenders

1 Tbsp. olive oil
4 chuck tender steaks, 1" thick
1 14.5-oz. can Italian style
     diced tomatoes, undrained
1 large onion, quartered & sliced
½ tsp. oregano
½ tsp. basil
½ tsp. garlic powder
¼ tsp. salt
¼ tsp. black pepper
1 16-oz. can navy beans,
     rinsed & drained
2 cups coarsely chopped fresh spinach
Shredded Parmesan cheese

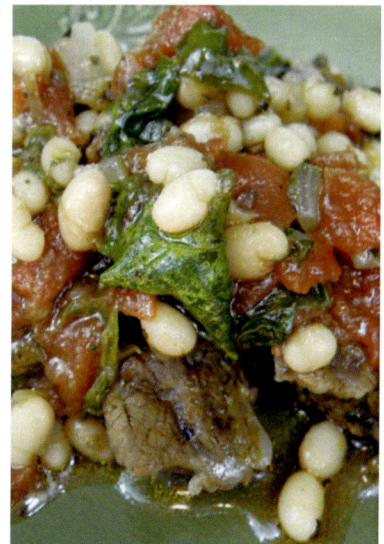

Heat oil in a Dutch oven.  Brown steaks on both sides.  Add tomatoes, onions, and seasonings. Bring to a boil. Reduce heat and tightly cover.  Simmer for 1½ hours to 1¾ hours, until steak is tender when pierced with a fork.  Remove steaks from pan and keep warm.  Stir beans into pan and bring to a boil.  Cook uncovered over medium heat for about 10 minutes, or until sauce has thickened.  Stir frequently.  Remove pan from heat and stir in spinach.  Let stand for 1 minute. Serve Italian sauce over steaks and sprinkle with Parmesan cheese.  Serves 4.

## Mock Stuffed Cabbage Casserole

1 lb. ground beef
1 large onion, chopped
1 green pepper, chopped
1½ cup Cauli-rice (page 168)
1½ cup cooked lentils
1 small head cabbage, coarsely chopped
1 10.75-oz. can tomato soup, undiluted
1 15-oz. can tomato sauce
　　(or a second can of tomato soup)
½ tsp. chili powder, optional
Salt and black pepper to taste

Brown ground beef and onion in a large non-stick skillet. Add green pepper and cook 3 minutes longer. Salt and pepper to taste. Drain. Add remaining ingredients. Pour mixture into a casserole dish. Bake uncovered at 350º for 45 minutes, or until hot and cabbage is cooked. Serves 8.

## Shipwreck Casserole

1 lb. ground beef
2 10.75-oz. cans tomato soup, undiluted
2 15-oz. cans kidney beans, rinsed & drained
1 1b. or 1 package parsnips,
　　peeled & chopped
½ tsp. salt
½ tsp. black pepper
2 cups celery, chopped
1 large onion, chopped
1 16-oz. can green beans, drained
1 Tbsp. Worcestershire sauce

Brown and drain ground beef. Place tomato soup and kidney beans in food processor and pulse a few times to barely chop beans. Set aside. Arrange parsnips in bottom of large casserole dish. Sprinkle with salt and pepper. Layer celery next. Spread half of soup/bean mixture. Layer on onions, then green beans. Mix remaining soup/bean mixture with Worcestershire sauce and ground beef. Spread over top. Cover and bake at 350º for 1½ hours. Let stand 10 minutes before serving. Serves 8.

Variation: replace green beans with chopped green pepper, chopped carrots, or favorite vegetable. Kidney beans can be stirred in whole instead of chopped.

## Country Cassoulet

1 lb. turkey breakfast sausage links
   or bulk sausage
2 stalks celery, diced
½ cup chopped onion
½ green pepper, chopped
2 cloves garlic, minced
½ tsp. salt
1 tsp. rubbed sage
1 16-oz. can lima beans, undrained
1 16-oz. can baked beans,
   rinsed & drained
1 8-oz. can baked beans, rinsed,
   drained, & pureed
¼-½ cup chicken broth
1 6-oz. can tomato paste

Cook sausage links in a non-stick skillet until brown and crisp. If using bulk sausage, crumble and cook until brown. Remove sausage from pan, leaving drippings in pan. Slice links if using. Set sausage aside. Add celery, onion, green pepper, and garlic to hot drippings and sauté until celery is tender. Add salt, sage, lima beans, baked beans, chicken broth (depending on thickness desired), tomato paste, and sausage. Simmer uncovered for 10 minutes, stirring occasionally. Serves 8.

Note: to puree beans, add some or all of the chicken broth to food processor with beans.

Variation: for an Italian flavor, replace turkey breakfast sausage with turkey Italian sausage. Replace sage with Italian seasoning.

## Chuckwagon Lentil Casserole

2 cups dried lentils, sorted & rinsed
1 quart water
1 lb. ground beef

Sauce:
1 cup ketchup
1 cup water
½ cup light olive oil
1 1.25-oz. packet dry onion soup mix
1 tsp. prepared yellow mustard
1 tsp. cider vinegar
¼ tsp. black pepper

Combine lentils and water in a saucepan. Bring to a boil. Reduce heat to medium and simmer uncovered for 30 minutes, or until tender (not mushy). Drain. Brown ground beef in a Dutch oven. Drain. Stir in lentils and sauce. Bake uncovered at 400° for 45 minutes. Serves 8.

**117**

## Navy Cassoulet

2 Tbsp. olive oil
1 20-oz. package (1.25 lbs.) Italian seasoned
   ground turkey
1½ cups water
2 tsp. chicken bouillon paste or 2 cubes chicken
   bouillon*
1 medium onion, quartered & thinly sliced
3 large carrots, peeled & diced
3 medium parsnips, peeled & diced
3 large cloves garlic, minced
1 14.5-oz. can diced tomatoes, drained
3 15-oz. cans navy beans, rinsed & drained
½ tsp. ground marjoram
  or 1 tsp. dried thyme leaf
½ tsp. salt
¼ tsp. black pepper

### Topping:

1 small can French-fried onions

In a heavy, oven proof, Dutch oven, heat oil over medium heat. Brown sausage in oil, crumbling while cooking. Add remaining ingredients, except topping. Mix well, scraping bottom of pan. Bring to a boil. Reduce heat to low. Cover and simmer for about 1 hour, until mixture thickens and vegetables are tender, stirring occasionally. Heat oven to 400°. Sprinkle onion topping over cassoulet. Place in oven and bake, uncovered, for 5-10 minutes or until onions are golden brown.
*Better than Bouillon™ is the bouillon paste recommended. If using bouillon cubes reduce or eliminate the salt as bouillon cubes contain more salt than the bouillon paste.

## Stove Top Hotdish

1 lb. ground beef
1 large onion, chopped
2 cloves garlic, minced
4 large carrots, peeled
4 cups shredded cabbage
2 15-oz. cans red beans, rinsed & drained
1 cup beef broth
1½ tsp. salt

Place carrots into a food processor and pulse to coarsely chop. In a Dutch oven, brown ground beef, onion, and garlic. Add remaining ingredients. Cover and cook over medium heat for 20 minutes, stirring occasionally. Serves 6.

Variations: replace beef broth with 1 cup water and 1 tsp. beef bouillon paste or 1 cube beef bouillon.* Season to taste by adding Italian seasoning, Cajun seasoning, black pepper, crushed red pepper, mushrooms, or any vegetable seasoning.
*Better than Bouillon™ is the bouillon paste recommended. If using bouillon cubes reduce or eliminate the salt as bouillon cubes contain more salt than the bouillon paste.

**118**

## Beef and Caramelized Onion Casserole

2 Tbsp. olive oil
3-4 lbs. stew meat or venison
    cut into 1-inch cubes
½ tsp. salt
½ tsp. black pepper
3 Tbsp. butter
4 large sweet onions, halved
    and thinly sliced
3 large cloves garlic, minced
2½ Tbsp. garbanzo bean flour
¾ cup water
2 tsp. beef bouillon paste or 2 cubes beef bouillon*
1 10.5-oz. can beef consommé
1 lb. baby carrots, julienned
1 Tbsp. Worcestershire sauce
1 medium bay leaf
¼ tsp. sage
1 15-oz. can black beans, rinsed & drained

### Topping:
1½ cups shredded mozzarella cheese

### "Pasta" options:
1 batch (bean flour) Gnocchi (page 180)
3 cups Cabbage Noodles (page 165)
3 cups Cauli-rice (page 168)

In a large Dutch oven, heat olive oil over medium-high heat. Sprinkle stew meat with salt and pepper, add to oil in batches, and brown well. Remove from pan and set aside. In same pot, melt butter. Add onions and cook over medium heat, stirring frequently, for 15-20 minutes or until onions are tender. Increase heat to medium-high and cook 3-4 minutes, or until onions are caramel color, stirring frequently. Stir in garlic and flour and cook for 1 minute while continuing to stir. Add water and bouillon, stirring until thickened, about 2 minutes. Add stew meat and remaining ingredients, except beans and cheese. Simmer uncovered for 45 minutes, stirring occasionally. Puree beans in a food processor. Add to meat mixture. Simmer for additional 15 minutes, stirring frequently. Remove bay leaf. Choose one of the pasta options to place in an oil-sprayed 9x13" casserole dish. Spoon meat mixture over "pasta" and sprinkle mozzarella cheese on top. Bake uncovered in preheated 350° oven for 5-10 minutes or until cheese has melted. Best if eaten immediately. Serves 10.

*Better than Bouillon™ is the bouillon paste recommended. If using bouillon cubes reduce or eliminate the salt as bouillon cubes contain more salt than the bouillon paste.

## Meatball Supper

2 Tbsp. butter
3 Tbsp. garbanzo bean flour
4 tsp. beef bouillon paste or 4 cubes beef
    bouillon*
2 cups water
4 cups frozen Swiss meatballs
1½ cups frozen sliced carrots
2 cups frozen green beans
2 Tbsp. diced onion
1 15-oz. can kidney beans,
    rinsed & drained

Melt butter in a Dutch oven.  Stir in flour.  Whisk in bouillon and water.  Bring to a boil.  Add meatballs, carrots, green beans, and onion.  Cook uncovered over medium heat for 15-20 minutes.  Gravy should begin to thicken.  Stir in kidney beans and cook 5 minutes longer.  Serves 10.

*Better than Bouillon™ is the bouillon paste recommended.  If using bouillon cubes recipe will be saltier.

## Goulash

1 lb. ground beef
1 large onion, chopped
2 stalks celery, chopped
1 14.5-oz. can diced tomatoes, drained
2 10.75-oz. cans tomato soup, undiluted
1 16-oz. can baby butter beans,
    rinsed & drained
1 tsp. paprika
½ tsp. garlic powder
¼ tsp. salt

In a Dutch oven, brown ground beef with onion, and celery.  Drain.  Add remaining ingredients.  Stir and heat through.  Bake uncovered at 350º for 30 minutes.  Serves 6.

Variation:  add another can of beans and/or 1 cup diced vegetables.

## Bean 'n'` Bacon Sloppy Joes

1 lb. ground beef
1 small onion, chopped
2 Tbsp. diced green pepper
1 11.25-oz. can bean with bacon soup,
    undiluted
⅓ cup ketchup
1 Tbsp. prepared yellow mustard
2 Tbsp. water

In a large non-stick skillet, brown ground beef with onion and green pepper. Drain. Add remaining ingredients. Heat to boiling. Serve with **Bean Flour Yeast Bread (page 171)** or in **Chickpea Tortillas (page 175).** Serves 3-4.

## BBQ'd Beef 'n' Ranch Beans

3 lb. beef or venison stew meat,
    cut into 1" cubes
1½ tsp. ground mustard
1 tsp. salt
1 tsp. paprika
½ tsp. chili powder
¼ tsp. black pepper
1 large onion, chopped
2 10-oz. cans diced tomatoes
    and green chilies
1 15-oz. can ranch-style or chili beans,
    undrained
1 16-oz. can baked beans,
    rinsed & drained
1 8-oz. can baked beans,
    rinsed, drained, & pureed
2 Tbsp. barbeque sauce

Place beef in a 3 quart slow cooker. Combine mustard, salt, paprika, chili powder, and pepper. Sprinkle onto beef and toss to coat. Mix together remaining ingredients and spread on top of stew meat. Cover and cook on low for 6-8 hours, until meat is tender. Serve topped with additional barbeque sauce. Serves 6-8.

## Chow Mein Bean Dish

1 lb. ground beef
1 tsp. salt
¼ tsp. black pepper
2 cups peeled & thinly sliced
    Daikon radishes
1 large onion, quartered & thinly sliced
1 15.5-oz. can great northern beans,
    rinsed & drained
1 10.5-oz. can cream of mushroom soup
⅓ soup can water
1 tsp. beef bouillon paste or 1 cube beef bouillon*
5 tsp. soy liquid aminos or soy sauce
2 tsp. Worcestershire sauce
1-2 cups diced celery
1 can chow mein vegetables, drained

Brown ground beef and drain. Sprinkle beef with salt and pepper. Mix half of beef with Daikon slices and place in bottom of a 9x13" casserole dish. Layer with onion slices, then beans. Whisk together soup, water, bouillon, liquid aminos, and Worcestershire sauce. Spread ½ of soup mixture over bean layer. Layer celery, chow mein vegetables, and remaining beef. Spread remaining soup mixture over top. Cover and bake at 350° for 1½ hours. Serves 10.

*Better than Bouillon™ is the bouillon paste recommended. If using bouillon cubes reduce or eliminate the salt as bouillon cubes contain more salt than the bouillon paste.

## Tomato Soup and Cauli-rice Hotdish

1 lb. ground beef
1 small onion, chopped
1 clove garlic, minced
2 10.75-oz. cans tomato soup, undiluted
1 16-oz. can navy or lima beans,
    rinsed & drained
2-3 cups Cauli-rice (page 168)
1 tsp. chili powder
Salt and black pepper to taste
1 cup shredded cheddar cheese

In a large skillet, brown hamburger, onion, and garlic. Drain. Add tomato soup and beans. Add **Cauli-rice** and chili powder. Salt and pepper to taste. Mix well. Transfer to a casserole dish. Cover and bake at 350° for 30-45 minutes, or until hot. Remove from oven and sprinkle with cheese. Return to oven and bake until cheese has melted, about 5 minutes. Serves 8-10.

## Creamy Dried Beef & Lima Casserole

2 2.5-oz. jars dried beef, shredded
⅓ cup butter
6 Tbsp. garbanzo bean flour
1 tsp. onion powder
½ tsp. dry ground mustard
¼ tsp. black pepper
2½ cups Almond Milk (page 107)
2 15-oz. cans green lima beans,
   rinsed & drained

Heat butter in a large non-stick skillet over medium heat. Add dried beef and cook for several minutes. Stir in bean flour, onion powder, mustard, and pepper. Pour in almond milk and stir well. Bring to a boil and continue cooking over medium heat, stirring constantly until thickened. This will take some time. Remove from heat and stir in beans. Pour into an oil-sprayed 2 quart casserole dish. Bake uncovered at 350º for 30-45 minutes, until hot and bubbly. Serves 6.

## Salmon & Lima Pea Casserole

¼ cup butter
⅓ cup diced red onion
⅓ cup diced celery
¼ cup diced green pepper
3 Tbsp. garbanzo bean flour
½ tsp. salt
½ tsp. black pepper
1 cup Almond Milk (page 107)
1 10.75-oz. can cream of chicken soup,
   undiluted
1 cup small curd cottage cheese
1 15-oz. can baby butter or lima beans,
   rinsed & drained
½ cup frozen peas, thawed
1 16-oz. can pink salmon, drained, skinned, & deboned
2 cups purchased French fried onions, divided

Heat butter in a large saucepan. Sauté onion, celery, and green pepper until tender. Add flour, salt, and pepper. Stir well. Add almond milk and soup. Bring mixture to a boil, stirring constantly. Remove from heat and stir in cottage cheese. Break salmon into small chunks and place into a medium bowl. Add lima beans and peas and mix well. Spray a 9x13" casserole dish with oil. Spread ½ of salmon mixture in dish and cover with ½ of soup mixture. Sprinkle with 1 cup French fried onions. Spread remaining salmon mixture over onions, then soup mixture over salmon, and top with remaining onions. Bake uncovered at 350º for 45 minutes, or until hot and bubbly. Serves 6.

## Zucchini Boats

2 medium zucchini (about 8" long)
2 Tbsp. olive oil
1 medium onion, chopped
1 clove garlic, minced
1 cup diced tomatoes
1 15-oz. can black or red beans,
    rinsed & drained
¼ cup sun-dried tomato pesto
¼-½ tsp. salt
2 Tbsp. grated Parmesan cheese
¼-½ cup diced pepperoni
    or cooked Italian sausage

### Topping:
1 cup shredded mozzarella cheese

Wash zucchini. Fill a large pot halfway with water. Place whole zucchini in water, bring to a boil. Boil for 2 minutes. Use tongs to transfer zucchini to a colander or plate until they are cool enough to handle. With a large knife, cut zucchini in half lengthwise. Scoop out the flesh with a spoon, being sure to leave an outer wall about ¼-⅓" thick. These will resemble a dugout canoe. Place boats onto a baking sheet and set aside. Dice zucchini flesh. Heat oil in a large non-stick skillet. Add onion and diced zucchini. Sauté over medium heat for 5 minutes, stirring constantly. Add garlic and sauté 2 more minutes. Add tomatoes, beans, tomato pesto, salt, Parmesan cheese, and pepperoni. Mix and continue cooking until hot, stirring constantly. Spoon filling into boats. Bake uncovered at 400° for 25 minutes. Remove and sprinkle each boat with ¼ cup mozzarella cheese. Return to oven and bake 5 more minutes, until cheese has melted. Eat shell and all. Makes 4 boats.

## Chickpea Chicken Pizza

1 recipe Chickpea Individual Pizza Crusts
    (page 174)

### Topping:
2 Tbsp. basil pesto
1 cup cooked chicken, cubed
3 slices provolone cheese

Place crusts onto an oil-sprayed baking sheet. Top each crust with pesto, chicken, and cheese torn to cover top. Bake in preheated oven at 400° for 10-15 minutes, until cheese has melted. Makes two 9" pizzas and serves 3-4.

## Blackened Chicken & Spinach Pizza

1 recipe Chickpea Individual Pizza Crusts (page 174)
1 boneless skinless chicken breast
3 tsp. blackened seasoning, divided
4 Tbsp. butter, divided
4 cloves garlic, minced
1 small onion, julienned
2 Tbsp. garbanzo bean flour
1 cup Almond Milk (page 107)
2 tsp. dried basil
1 ½ cups shredded mozzarella cheese,
     divided
1 cup spinach leaves, de-stemmed
¼ cup grated Parmesan cheese

### Blackened Seasoning:
1½ tsp. paprika
1¼ tsp. salt
½ tsp. onion powder
½ tsp. garlic powder
¾ tsp. black pepper
¼ tsp. cayenne pepper
¼ tsp. dried thyme
¼ tsp. dried oregano

Mix together seasoning. Pound chicken breast to 1/4" thickness. Using 2 tsp. seasoning, sprinkle top and bottom of chicken breast . Reserve remaining seasoning for another use. Heat 2 Tbsp. butter in a large non-stick skillet over medium heat. Add chicken and cook about 3 minutes per side or until chicken is done. Remove from heat. Cut chicken into thin strips and set aside. Melt remaining 2 Tbsp. butter in same skillet. Add garlic and onion and sauté for 2 minutes. Stir in flour and almond milk. Whisk continuously for 5 minutes, until thickened. Stir in basil and remaining 1 tsp. seasoning. Remove from heat. Place pizza crusts on an oil-sprayed baking sheet. Spread sauce evenly over crusts. Sprinkle each crust with ½ cup mozzarella cheese and layer with spinach leaves and chicken strips. Top each pizza with ¼ cup mozzarella and 2 Tbsp. Parmesan cheese. Bake at 450° for 15 minutes. Serves 3-4.

Variation:  toppings can be divided over 3 crusts if you prefer less topping.

## Enchilada Chicken Pizza

**1 recipe Chickpea Individual Pizza Crusts (page 174)**

**Topping:**
**⅔ cup chopped onion**
**1 Tbsp. olive oil**
**2 cups cubed cooked chicken**
**1 4-oz. can chopped green chilies**
**2 Tbsp. taco seasoning**
**½ cup enchilada sauce**
**1 cup shredded mozzarella cheese**
**1 cup shredded Mexican cheese blend**

Boil chicken for 20 minutes to cook. Cube when cool. In a large skillet, sauté onion in oil for 3-4 minutes, until tender. Add chicken, green chilies, and taco seasoning. Cook 2-3 minutes, until heated through. Spread enchilada sauce over the 2 crusts. Sprinkle each pizza with mozzarella cheese and evenly distribute chicken mixture. Top with Mexican cheese. Bake at 400º for 10 minutes or until cheese has melted. Makes 2 pizzas and serves 3-4.

## Taco Pizza

**1 recipe Chickpea Individual Pizza Crusts**
   **(page 174)**
**½ lb. ground beef**
**½ cup thick salsa**
**2 tsp. taco seasoning**
**1 cup Delicious Refried Beans, divided**
   **(page150)**
**½ cup shredded cheddar cheese, divided**
**2 small tomatoes, diced**
**½ small onion, diced**
**Shredded romaine lettuce**
**Sour cream**
**Taco sauce**

Place both pizza crusts on an oil-sprayed baking sheet. Brown ground beef and drain. Mix salsa and taco seasoning into beef. Spread ½ cup of refried beans over each crust. Spoon half of beef mixture over each pizza. Bake at 400º for 10 minutes. Remove from oven and top with cheese, tomatoes, onion, lettuce, sour cream, and taco sauce. Makes 2 pizzas and serves 3-4.

## Broiled Red Onion Pizza

1 recipe Chickpea Individual Pizza Crusts
   (page 174)

**Toppings:**
2 Tbsp. olive oil, divided
1 medium red onion, quartered & sliced
3 cloves garlic, minced
½ cup diced fresh tomatoes
½ cup diced green peppers
1 4-oz. can chopped black olives
1 tsp. oregano
¼ cup mozzarella cheese, shredded or cubed

Heat 1 Tbsp. oil in a large non-stick skillet. Add red onion and sauté for 10 minutes, until tender. Remove onion from pan and set aside. Add remaining 1 tsp. oil to skillet and heat. Add garlic, tomatoes, peppers, olives, and oregano. Sauté for 2 minutes. Mix in red onions. Spoon half of mixture over each crust. Top with cheese. If using cubes, press them in slightly. Place pizzas onto a broiler pan or broiler-proof baking sheet. Place under broiler for 3-6 minutes, until cheese melts. Makes 2 pizzas and serves 3-4.

## Polka Dot Meatza

1 lb. lean ground beef
1 tsp. salt
1 15-oz. can black or kidney beans, rinsed & drained
1 10.5-oz. can tomato soup, undiluted
2 cups shredded cheddar cheese, divided
1 large onion, chopped
2 Tbsp. butter
6 oz. all beef ring sausage or ring bologna

Place double layer of foil on a baking sheet. Turn up edges of foil to catch grease. Spray foil. Mix together ground beef and salt. Pat firmly on foil to form 12" circle. Heat butter in skillet and sauté onion until tender. Place tomato soup, onion, and beans in food processor and pulse to coarsely chop. Spread mixture on top of ground beef. Sprinkle with 1 cup cheese. Dot with pepperoni. Bake at 450° for 25 minutes. Spoon or drain off fat. Sprinkle remaining cheese on top and continue baking 5 minutes, or until cheese has melted. Serves 4.

## Meat Crust Italian Pizza

### Crust:
1¼ lbs. ground beef
½ tsp. crushed fennel seed
½ tsp. basil
½ tsp. oregano
½ tsp. garlic powder
½ tsp. salt
1 tsp. dried minced onion
⅓ cup grated Parmesan cheese

### Toppings:
½ cup pizza sauce
1 medium green pepper, finely chopped
½ small sweet onion, finely chopped
2 Tbsp. chopped black olives
2 cups shredded mozzarella and
    provolone blend cheese
1 cup shredded cheddar cheese
Pepperoni slices (optional)

Mix all crust ingredients together and divide in half. Spray a 10" or 11" skillet with oil and pat half of the crust mixture in the bottom of pan. Crust should be thin. Fry uncovered over medium heat until the bottom is browned, about 8 minutes. Do not flip. Holding crust with spatula, drain off grease. Loosen crust and slide onto a large baking sheet. Repeat with other half of crust mixture. Pat grease off of top of crusts with paper towel if necessary. Divide toppings over both pizzas. Bake at 400° for 15-20 minutes or until cheese is melted but not brown. Makes two 10"or 11" pizzas and serves 4-5.

Variation: add toppings of your choice—tomatoes, pepperoni, zucchini, spinach, etc.

# Burgers, Patties, & Loaves

## Notes about Bean Burgers

Bean burgers, patties, and loaf slices are best fried in a combination of butter and olive oil. Olive oil gives them a crispiness and butter enhances the flavors.

Bean burgers will be moist when pattied and during frying. Make them a little thinner than a hamburger. Flip burgers carefully so they do not fall apart. They will firm up slightly when cooled.

Bean burgers and patties are best with a sauce or dip.

Bean burgers and patties freeze well. To reheat, place in microwave, or bake at 350° for 10 minutes on a baking sheet.

For an on-the-go snack, make any bean burgers nugget-sized, and place into a zipper-style bag. Nuggets are good, hot or cold.

## Lentil Burgers

3 cups water
1 cup dried lentils, sorted & rinsed
2 Tbsp.+2 tsp. soy liquid aminos or soy sauce,
   divided
2 large cloves garlic, minced
1 medium onion, minced
1 large carrot, coarse ground
   in blender or food processor
1 egg, beaten
¼ cup oat bran, ground in blender
½ cup garbanzo bean flour
½ tsp. thyme
½ tsp. marjoram
1 tsp. Vege-Sal® or seasoning salt
Butter for frying

Bring water to a boil. Add lentils, 2 Tbsp. liquid aminos, and garlic. Simmer on low for 30 minutes. Lentils should retain shape but mash when pressed. Drain lentils in a colander. Place remaining ingredients, including 2 tsp. of liquid aminos into a large bowl. Add lentils and mix well. Heat butter in a non-stick skillet. Using a tablespoon, scoop out a spoonful of mixture. Press mixture slightly on the side of the bowl to pack it. Drop each spoonful of mixture into skillet. Press each spoonful lightly with a fork to pack and shape into burgers. Each burger should be approximately 2" in diameter. Fry in batches over medium heat, adding butter to skillet for each new batch. Brown well on both sides. Makes about 4 dozen.

## Lentil Walnut Burgers

2 Tbsp. olive oil
1 cup onion, minced
4 large cloves garlic, minced
1¾ cup cooked lentils
1 small egg (or 1 large egg white), beaten
2 Tbsp. apple cider vinegar
2 Tbsp. chopped ripe olives
½ cup walnuts, finely chopped
1 tsp. salt
1 tsp. dry mustard
¼ tsp. black pepper
¼ cup oat bran
2 Tbsp. garbanzo bean flour
2 Tbsp. oil for frying
2 Tbsp. butter for frying

Heat olive oil in large non-stick skillet. Sauté onions and garlic over low heat until tender. Place onion mixture in bowl and add remaining ingredients. Mix well. Chill for 1 hour. Heat oil and butter in skillet. Using ¼ cup measure, scoop out mixture and form into burgers. They will be sticky. Fry on medium-low heat until brown and crisp, flipping carefully to brown both sides. Burgers will firm up when done. For cheese burgers, add slices of cheese, cover pan and cook on low until cheese melts. Makes 12 burgers.

## Zesty White Bean Burgers

### Burgers:
1 15.5-oz. can Great Northern beans,
    rinsed & drained
1 4-oz. can diced mild green chilies
2 medium green onions, chopped
½-1 cup oat bran
1 egg
2 Tbsp. olive oil for frying
2 Tbsp. butter for frying

### Topping:
8 slices pepper jack cheese

Place all burger ingredients into a food processor and pulse until mixed and coursely chopped. Using a ¼ cup measure, form into patties. Heat oil and butter in a large non-stick skillet. Fry burgers, flipping once to brown on both sides. Place cheese slice on each burger, cover pan, and heat on low until cheese has melted. Makes 8-9 burgers.

**131**

## Jicama Split Pea Burgers

4 Tbsp. butter, divided
2 Tbsp. olive oil, divided
1 small onion, shredded
1 carrot, peeled & shredded
½ cup shredded jicama
1 clove garlic, minced
½ tsp. Vege Sal® or seasoning salt
1 egg, beaten
¼ cup oat bran
1-1¼ cups cooked split peas or lentils
    (tender but not mushy)

In a large non-stick skillet, melt 2 Tbsp. butter and 1 Tbsp. olive oil. Sauté onion, carrot, jicama, and garlic for 2-3 minutes. Pour into a bowl. Add seasoning salt, egg, oat bran, and split peas. Mix well. Heat remaining butter and oil in skillet over medium heat. Using a ¼ cup measure, form into burgers. Patties will be very moist and slightly loose. Brown completely on one side before flipping and browning other side. Makes 10 burgers.

## Cajun 'Banzo Burgers

½ medium onion, chopped
1 large carrot, chopped
2 cloves garlic, minced
2 tsp. Cajun seasoning
1 tsp. celery salt
½ cup walnuts
1 15.5-oz. can garbanzo beans,
    rinsed & drained
¼ cup oat bran
1 egg, beaten
2 Tbsp. olive oil for frying, divided
2 Tbsp. butter for frying

Pulse onion, carrot, and garlic in food processor until coarse crumbs. Heat 1 Tbsp. oil in large non-stick skillet. Add onion mixture, Cajun seasoning, and celery salt. Sauté until carrots are tender-crisp. Place onion mixture into a bowl. Pulse walnuts in food processor until crumbly and add to onion mixture. Place garbanzo beans in food processor and pulse until coarsely chopped. Add to onion mixture. Add oat bran and egg. Mix well. Using a ¼ cup measure, form into patties. Heat remaining oil and butter in same skillet. Fry burgers over medium heat. Brown well on both sides. Let sit a few minutes to firm up. Makes 8-10 burgers.

## Red Bean Jalapeño Burgers

1 Tbsp. olive oil
½ medium onion, diced
½ cup Roma tomatoes, chopped (drain juice)
1 tsp. minced jalapeño peppers
    or ¼ tsp. red pepper flakes
1 clove garlic, minced
1 tsp. chili powder
1 15-oz. can red kidney beans,
    rinsed & drained
¼ cup oat bran
2 Tbsp. barbecue sauce
1 large egg white, slightly beaten
1 Tbsp. olive oil for frying
1 Tbsp. butter for frying

Heat 1 Tbsp. olive oil in a small saucepan. Add onion, tomato, jalapeño, garlic, and chili powder. Sauté 5 minutes. Cool slightly. Using a fork or food processor, coarsely mash beans and pour into a bowl. Add onion mixture and remaining ingredients. Mix well. Let stand for 15 minutes. Using a ¼ cup measure, divide mixture and shape into patties. Heat 1 Tbsp. each of oil and butter in a large non-stick skillet. Place patties into skillet and fry over medium heat until browned on both sides, flipping carefully. Burgers will be soft but will firm up after a couple of minutes. Serve with barbeque sauce if desired. These can be made ahead of time and chilled until ready to fry. Makes 9 burgers.

## Salsa Black Bean Burgers

1 15-oz. can black beans, rinsed & drained
½ medium sweet or red onion, finely chopped
2 Tbsp. chunky salsa (drain if necessary)
¼-½ tsp. red pepper sauce (hot sauce)
¼ cup oat bran
1 tsp. taco seasoning
¼ tsp. salt
1 Tbsp. olive oil for frying
1 Tbsp. butter for frying

Using a fork or food processor, coarsely mash beans. Pour into bowl and add onion, salsa, red pepper sauce, oat bran, taco seasoning and salt. Mix well. Let stand for 15 minutes. Using a ¼ cup measure, divide mixture and shape into patties. Heat oil and butter in large skillet. Place patties into skillet and fry over medium heat until browned on both sides, flipping carefully. Burgers will be soft but will firm up after a couple of minutes. Serve plain or with ¼ cup warmed salsa over each burger. These can be made ahead of time and chilled until ready to fry. Makes 8 burgers.

**133**

## Jalapeño Black Bean & Lentil Cheeseburgers

**Burgers:**
1 15-oz. can black beans,
   rinsed & drained
1½ cups cooked lentils
   (about ¾ cup dried)
½ small onion
3 cloves garlic
2 seeded jalapeño peppers
2 tsp. chili powder
2 tsp. salt
1 tsp. black pepper
2 beaten eggs
¼ cup oat bran
¼ cup garbanzo bean flour

**Topping:**
Jalapeño pepper cheese slices
3 Tbsp. olive oil for frying
3 Tbsp. butter for frying

Place onion, garlic and jalapeño peppers into a food processor. Pulse until finely chopped. Add beans and lentils and pulse until beans are coarsely mashed and mixed with onion mixture. Do not puree. Place bean mixture into a bowl and add remaining burger ingredients. Heat 1 Tbsp. oil and 1 Tbsp. butter in a large non-stick skillet for each of 3 batches. Using a ¼ cup measure, scoop out mixture and form into patties. These will be sticky. Fry in skillet over medium-low heat until browned and crisp on both sides, flipping carefully. Do not flip too soon or burgers will fall apart. Cook slowly. Add cheese slices. Cover and cook on low until cheese melts. Burgers will be soft but will firm up after a couple of minutes. Makes 12 burgers.

## Oriental Bean Patties with Horseradish Sauce

**Patties:**
1 15-oz. can red kidney beans,
   rinsed & drained
¼ cup oat bran
4 green onions, finely chopped
1 small clove garlic, minced
1 small egg (or 1 large egg white)
2 tsp. soy liquid aminos or soy sauce
½ tsp. ground ginger
1 Tbsp. olive oil for frying
1 Tbsp. butter for frying

**Sauce:**
½ cup mayonnaise
2 Tbsp. prepared horseradish
2 green onions, finely chopped
2 tsp. soy liquid aminos or soy sauce

Coarsely mash kidney beans in a large bowl. Mix in remaining patty ingredients. Heat oil and butter together in a large non-stick skillet. Form mixture into 4-8 patties, depending on how large you would like them. Cook patties over medium heat until browned and crispy on both sides. Flip only once so patties do not fall apart. Allow to sit a few minutes to firm up. Combine sauce ingredients and serve on top of patties. Serves 4-6.

Variation: top with chopped cucumbers.

## Jamaican Rice and Bean Burgers

1 Tbsp. olive oil
1 large onion, chopped
1 large sweet red pepper, chopped
3 cloves garlic, minced
1 tsp. ginger
¾ tsp. allspice
¼ tsp. salt
¼ tsp. crushed red pepper,
　 or more to taste
⅓ cup oat bran
1 egg
1 15-oz. can black beans,
　 rinsed & drained
1 cup Cauli-rice (page 168)
1 Tbsp. olive oil for frying
2 Tbsp. butter for frying

Heat 1 Tbsp. olive oil in large non-stick skillet. Add onion, red peppers, and garlic. Saute 5-7 minutes, until tender-crisp. Add all spices and stir well. Place onion mixture into food processor with oat bran, egg, and black beans. Pulse several times until medium chopped, not a paste. Place bean mixture into bowl and fold in **Cauli-rice**. Using a ¼ cup measure, form into patties. Heat remaining oil and butter in same skillet. Fry burgers in batches. Brown well on both sides over medium heat. Let sit a few minutes to firm up. Makes 12-18 burgers.

## Cowboy Burgers

### Burgers:

½ cup cooked kidney or black beans,
   rinsed & drained
1 lb. ground beef or turkey
6 Tbsp. barbecue sauce
4 tsp. prepared white horseradish
4-5 cloves garlic, minced
½ small onion, diced
½ tsp. salt
½ tsp. black pepper
½ tsp. ground mustard
¼ cup oat bran
1 Tbsp. olive oil for frying
2 Tbsp. butter for frying

### Sauce:

¼ cup mayonnaise
2 Tbsp. barbecue sauce
1 Tbsp. prepared white horseradish

Mash beans and mix with remaining burger ingredients. Using a ¼ cup measure, shape mixture into patties. Heat oil and butter in a large non-stick skillet. Fry over medium to medium-low heat. Watch carefully as the barbecue sauce will cause the burgers to burn if cooked on too high a setting. Mix sauce ingredients together and serve on burgers. Makes 10-15 burgers.

Variation:  make burgers larger and grill. Spray each side of burger with an oil cooking spray and grill 5-6 minutes per side.

## Asian Cauli-rice and Lentil Patties

### Patties:

¾ cup unflavored Cauli-rice (page 168)
½ cup cooked lentils, slightly mashed
¼ cup finely chopped cashews or peanuts
2 Tbsp. oat bran
1 Tbsp. garbanzo bean flour
2 Tbsp. stir-fry sauce
4 medium green onions, finely chopped
1 egg, beaten

### Vegetable sauce:

1 stalk celery, sliced
1 large carrot, peeled & sliced
½ cup water
2 Tbsp. stir-fry sauce

**136**

Mix all patty ingredients together and shape into 5 or 6 patties. Heat olive oil in a large non-stick skillet. Cook patties about 10 minutes, turning once, until golden brown on both sides. Remove patties and keep warm. Heat vegetable sauce ingredients in the same skillet. Bring to boil and cook 5-10 minutes, stirring occasionally, until vegetables are tender-crisp and liquid is starting to be absorbed by vegetables. Serve sauce over patties, or on side dishes. Serves 4-6.

## Lentil Curry Patties with Curry Sauce

### Curry Sauce:
1 cup mayonnaise
1 tsp. curry powder
2 Tbsp. finely minced onion
1 Tbsp. lemon juice

### Patties:
4 large radishes, quartered
1 medium red onion, quartered
1 large clove garlic, sliced
1 tsp. fresh chopped ginger
   or ½ tsp. dried ginger
3 cups cooked lentils
1 ½ tsp. curry powder
1 tsp. salt
1 tsp. black pepper
1 egg
⅓ cup oat bran
1 Tbsp. olive oil for frying
2 Tbsp. butter for frying

Mix together sauce ingredients and chill. Place radishes, red onion, garlic, and ginger in food processor and pulse until chopped. Add remaining ingredients and pulse to coarsely chop and mix. Heat oil and butter in a large non-stick skillet. Scoop heaping tablespoonfuls of mixture and form into patties approximately 1½" diameter. Fry on both sides until brown, over medium heat. Serve with curry sauce for dipping. Curry sauce is also excellent with vegetables. Makes about 50 patties.

## Stir-Fry Bean Burgers

1¼ cups frozen stir-fry vegetables, thawed
2-3 cloves garlic
1 egg
⅓-½ cup oat bran
½ tsp. salt
½ tsp. black pepper
1 tsp. dried onion flakes
1 15.5-oz. can Great Northern beans,
   rinsed & drained
1 Tbsp. olive oil for frying
2 Tbsp. butter for frying

Place vegetables and garlic into a food processor.  Pulse until finely chopped.  Add remaining ingredients and pulse until mixed and coarsely chopped.  Using a ¼ cup measure, scoop out bean mixture and form into patties.  Heat oil and butter in a large non-stick skillet.  Fry burgers over medium heat until browned on both sides, flipping carefully.  Allow to stand a couple of minutes to firm up.  Makes 9-10 burgers.

## Drive-In Walnut Burgers

1 cup chopped walnuts
1 15.5-oz. can garbanzo beans,
   rinsed & drained
⅓ cup oat bran
1 tsp. salt
1 tsp. black pepper
1 tsp. garlic powder
¼ tsp. crushed red pepper flakes
1 Tbsp. apple cider vinegar
1 Tbsp. extra virgin olive oil
1 egg
1 Tbsp. olive oil for frying
1 Tbsp. butter for frying
Bean Flour Yeast Bread (page 171)
Lettuce, tomato, avocado,
   and honey mustard

Place all burger ingredients into a food processor and pulse until mixed and just coarsely chopped.  Using a ¼ cup measure, form into 8 patties.  Heat oil and butter in a large non-stick skillet.  Fry burgers, flipping once to brown on both sides.  Serve on **Bean Flour Bread** with lettuce, tomato, avocado, and honey mustard.  Makes 8 burgers.

Note:  burgers are also great grilled.  Make patties a little larger and place onto an oiled grill.  Grill about 4 minutes per side, flipping carefully.

**138**

## Tex-Mex Bean Burger

1 chipotle chili in adobo sauce
1 tsp. adobo sauce from can
2 Tbsp. (½ can) mild chopped green chilies
½-¾ tsp. chili powder, to taste
½ tsp. salt
⅓ cup oat bran
1 egg
1 15-oz. can black beans, rinsed & drained
½ cup Cauli-rice (page 168)
1 Tbsp. olive oil for frying
2 Tbsp. butter for frying

### Topping:
**Pepper jack cheese**

Open chipotle chili with a knife. Scrape out and discard seeds. Place chipotle chili, sauce, green chilies, chili powder, salt, oat bran, and egg into a food processor. Process until chilies are finely chopped. Add beans and pulse to coarsely chop. Pour mixture into a bowl and fold in **Cauli-rice**. Heat oil and butter in a large non-stick skillet. Using a ¼ cup measure, scoop out bean mixture and form into patties. Fry over medium heat until browned on both sides. Top with pepper jack cheese. Cover and cook on low until the cheese has melted. Top with **Chipotle Mayonnaise (below)** or sour cream and diced tomatoes. Serves 7.

Note: to store leftover chipotle chilies, line a baking sheet with parchment paper and lay chilies out with spaces between them. Scrape sauce out into a mound also. Place baking sheet in freezer until chilies are frozen. Remove from freezer and cut parchment to divide chilies. Place frozen chilies, still on individual papers into freezer-style zipper bag. Squeeze out air, seal, and freeze. Seeds can be scraped out before freezing or just before using.

## Chipotle Mayonnaise

⅔ cup mayonnaise
⅓ cup sour cream
⅓ cup chipotle salsa (thick)
1 tsp. lime juice

Mix all ingredients together. Use as a spread or a dip for bean burgers. Makes 1⅓ cups.

## Spinach Bean Burgers

1½ cups fresh spinach
1 16-oz. can navy beans, rinsed & drained
1 cup cooked lentils
⅓ cup oat bran
½ medium onion, chopped
1 egg
1 tsp. Vege Sal® or seasoning salt
2 tsp. crushed red pepper flakes
3 tsp. garlic powder
2 Tbsp. olive oil for frying
2 Tbsp. butter for frying

Pulse spinach in a food processor until chopped. Add remaining ingredients. Pulse until coarsely chopped and mixed. Using a ¼ cup measure, scoop out bean mixture and form into burgers. In a non-stick skillet, heat 1 Tbsp. oil and 1 Tbsp. butter. Fry burgers in two batches over medium heat until browned, flipping once to brown both sides. Add remaining oil and butter for second batch. Serve with ranch dressing, dill dip, or sauce of choice. Makes 12-15 burgers.

## Red Bean Chickpea Nuggets

1 15.5-oz. can red beans, rinsed & drained
1 15.5-oz. can garbanzo beans (chickpeas),
    rinsed & drained
1 large carrot, chopped
1 medium onion, chopped
1 clove garlic, minced
½ cup fresh parsley, chopped
2 Tbsp. raw sunflower seeds
2 Tbsp. tahini (sesame seed paste)
2 tsp. vegetable bouillon paste or 2 cubes
    vegetable bouillon*
2 eggs
¼ cup almond meal
¼ cup oat bran
1 Tbsp. oil for frying
2 Tbsp. butter for frying

Place all ingredients, except oil and butter, into a food processor. Pulse until well blended and coursely chopped. Scoop out 1 Tbsp. at a time. Form each spoonful into a nugget shape. Add another ¼ cup of oat bran if mixture is too thin to shape. Heat oil and butter in a large non-stick skillet. Fry nuggets over medium heat, flipping once to brown both sides. Makes about 40 nuggets and serves 8.

*Better than Bouillon™ is the bouillon paste recommended. If using bouillon cubes nuggets will be saltier.

**140**

## Dilly Lentil Rolls

½ cup almonds
2 cups cooked lentils
1 large onion, chopped
1 medium carrot, cut up
½ cup cottage cheese
½ tsp. Vege Sal® or seasoning salt
2 Tbsp. dry dill weed, divided

### Topping:
Dill dip (purchased)

Place almonds into a food processor and pulse to a meal, almost a flour. Pour into a bowl. Place lentils into food processor and puree. Scrape lentils into bowl with almonds. Pulse onion and carrot in food processor until finely chopped (not pureed). Add to lentils. Mix in cottage cheese, Vege Sal® and 1 Tbsp. dill weed. Mix well. Using a ¼ cup measure, make into 10 mini loaves. Place onto an oil-sprayed or parchment lined baking sheet. Sprinkle remaining dill weed evenly over rolls. Bake at 400° for 30 minutes. Serve hot topped with a purchased dill dip. Serves 10.

## Cheddar Lima Loaf

½ cup pecans
¼ cup oat bran
1 15-oz. can large lima beans,
    rinsed & drained
½ cup chopped onion
1 carrot, chopped
2 eggs, beaten
½ cup Almond Milk (page 107)
1½ cups shredded sharp cheddar cheese
½ tsp. salt
½ tsp. garlic powder

Place pecans into a food processor and pulse to a meal, almost a flour. Pour into a large bowl. Add oat bran. Puree lima beans in food processor, scraping sides several times. Add beans to pecan mixture. Place onion and carrot in food processor and pulse to coarsely chop. Add onion mixture to pecan mixture and stir. Add remaining ingredients and mix well. Pour lima mixture into an oil-sprayed loaf pan. Pan will be half full. Place loaf pan in a larger pan and add 1" of water to outer pan. Bake at 350° for 1 hour and 15 minutes, or until a knife inserted in center comes out clean. Slice and serve. Chill leftovers. Slice and fry in butter to reheat. Serves 6-8.

## Sausage Lentil Loaf

1 lb. dry lentils, sorted & rinsed
1-1½ cups walnuts, pecans,
   or a mix of both
½ cup raw sunflower seeds
1 egg, beaten
2-2½ tsp. salt
1 tsp. black pepper
1 Tbsp. sage
½ tsp. allspice

Place lentils into a soup pot. Cover with water. Bring to a boil. Reduce heat and simmer 30 minutes, or until tender. Drain. Place lentils into a bowl and set aside. Pour nuts and sunflower seeds into a food processor. Grind to a meal (almost a flour) and add to lentils. (For a more moist loaf use 1 cup of nuts, and 1½ cups for a drier loaf.) Add remaining ingredients. Mix together, using hands to mash lentils. Pour mixture into a parchment lined loaf pan. Press into place with a spatula and smooth top. Bake uncovered at 350° for 1 hour and 15 minutes to 1 hour and 30 minutes, until a knife inserted in the center comes out clean. Allow to stand 5-10 minutes. Remove from pan and slice. To reheat, fry slices in butter. Serves 10.

Variation: make mixture into nugget-sized sausage patties and fry in butter until crisp.

Note: Although the recipe name implies there is sausage in the ingredients, there is none. The recipe tastes like a breakfast sausage, hence the name.

## Split Pea Roast

½ cup oat bran
½ cup water
1 Tbsp. beef bouillon paste or 3 cubes beef
   bouillon*
1 cup diced celery
½ cup diced green pepper
1 Tbsp. diced onion
2 Tbsp. butter, melted
½ tsp. basil
½ tsp. dill weed
¼ tsp. Vege Sal® or seasoning salt
1 cup almonds, coarsely ground
2 cups cooked split peas

Combine oat bran, hot water, and bouillon. Set aside to absorb. In a large mixing bowl combine celery, green pepper, onion, and butter. Add remaining ingredients. Mix in oat bran mixture and stir well. Spread mixture into an oil-sprayed casserole dish. Press into place with a spatula and smooth top. Bake uncovered at 350° for 1 hour, or until a knife inserted in center comes out clean. Serves 6-8.

*Better than Bouillon™ is the bouillon paste recommended. If using bouillon cubes recipe will be saltier.

## No-Bake Split Pea Loaf

3 Tbsp. butter
1 Tbsp. extra virgin olive oil
1½ cups chopped celery
1 cup chopped onion
3 large cloves garlic, minced
3 cups cooked split peas, mashed
4 tsp. soy liquid aminos or soy sauce
½ tsp. Vege Sal® or seasoning salt
1 tsp. sage

Heat oil and butter in a large non-stick skillet. Add celery, onion, and garlic and sauté until tender. Add split peas, liquid aminos, Vege Sal®, and sage. Mix well. Pour into a parchment lined loaf pan. Press into place with a spatula and smooth top. Chill for several hours. Slice and heat in microwave or fry in butter. This is a soft loaf. Serves 8.

## Tomato Lentil Loaf

1 lb. dried lentils, sorted & rinsed
2 Tbsp. butter
1 Tbsp. olive oil
½ cup chopped onion
½ cup chopped celery
2 cloves garlic, minced
1 10.75-oz. can tomato soup, undiluted
1 6-oz. can tomato paste
1 egg, beaten
1 tsp. salt
1 tsp. paprika

Cook lentils according to directions on **page 15**. Puree half of lentils in food processor or mash with potato masher. Pour all lentils into a large mixing bowl and set aside. Heat butter and oil in a large non-stick skillet. Sauté onion, celery, and garlic until tender. Scrape onion mixture and butter from pan into lentils. Stir well. Add remaining ingredients and mix well. Pour lentil mixture into a parchment lined loaf pan. Press into place with a spatula and smooth top. Pan will be full. Bake uncovered at 350º for 1¼ hours to 1½ hours, or until knife inserted in center comes out clean. Allow to stand for 10 minutes. Remove from pan and slice. This loaf will be moist. Serves 4.

Variation: line muffin tins with muffin papers. Spoon mixture into tins and bake at 350º for 50 minutes, or until a knife inserted in center comes out clean. Makes 18-20 muffins.

## Vegetable Lentil Loaf

¾ cup oat bran
½ cup hot water or beef broth
¾ cup walnuts, crumbled in food processor
2 medium carrots, coarsely chopped
   in food processor
1 small onion, chopped
2 stalks celery, chopped
1 small zucchini, diced
2 cloves garlic, minced
2 cups cooked lentils
2 eggs
1 tsp. Vege Sal® or seasoning salt
¼ tsp. oregano
¼ tsp. sage
¼ tsp. marjoram
½ tsp. thyme
½ cup ketchup

Mix hot water or broth with oat bran and let stand while preparing other ingredients. Combine all ingredients including oat bran mixture. Mix well. Line a quart-size loaf pan with parchment paper. Pour mixture into pan. Press in place with a spatula and smooth top. Bake uncovered at 350º for 1-1½ hours, until set. Remove loaf from pan and slice. This loaf will be moist. Serves 10.

## Four Bean Loaf

1 cup cooked black beans
1 cup cooked kidney beans
2 cups cooked garbanzo beans
1 14.5-oz. can cut green beans,
   drained & chopped
1 4-oz. can mushrooms, drained & chopped
½ cup pecans
2 stalks celery, chopped
1 medium onion, chopped
1 Tbsp. paprika
1 tsp. Vege Sal® or seasoning salt
¼ cup oat bran
1 Tbsp. soy liquid aminos or soy sauce
1 Tbsp. extra virgin olive oil
1 egg

In a food processor, coarsely chop black, kidney, and garbanzo beans. Pour into a large bowl. Coarsely chop green beans and mushrooms in food processor and add to bowl. Also chop celery and onions and add to bowl. Place pecans into food processor, pulse into small crumbles, and add to bowl. Stir until well blended. Pour mixture into a loaf pan lined with parchment paper. Pan will be full. Press into place with a spatula and smooth top. Bake uncovered at 375° for 50 minutes or until knife inserted in center comes out clean. Let cool 5-10 minutes before slicing.

Variation: replace beans with 4 cups of your choice of beans. If using canned beans, rinse and drain them before adding. Serves 8.

## Chili Loaf Casserole

**Loaf crust:**
2 lbs. lean ground beef
1 small onion, diced
½ cup oat bran
2 eggs
1 Tbsp. chili powder
½ tsp. salt

**"Potato" topping:**
2 15-oz. cans cannellini beans,
   rinsed & drained
2 tsp. beef bouillon paste or 2 cubes beef
   bouillon*
½ tsp. sage
½ tsp. black pepper
1 small onion, chopped
1 large clove garlic, minced
1 medium bay leaf
1 15-oz. can kidney beans,
   rinsed & drained
2 cups shredded cheddar
   or Mexican blend cheese, divided

Combine crust ingredients in a bowl and mix well. Press into an ungreased 9x13" casserole dish. Press loaf mixture thickly on bottom and up the sides of pan, leaving a hollow in the middle. Crust should resemble a thick rectangular pie crust. Bake at 375° for 25 minutes or until no longer pink. Drain if necessary. While crust is baking, place cannellini beans, bouillon, sage, and pepper into a food processor. Sauté onion, garlic, and bay leaf in butter, stirring constantly, until onion is tender. Discard bay leaf. Add onion mixture to bean mixture in food processor. Puree until smooth. Pour "potato" mixture into a bowl and fold in kidney beans. When loaf crust is done, remove from oven and layer 1 cup of cheese on crust. Spread "potato" mixture over cheese. Bake for 15 minutes or until "potato" layer is heated through. Sprinkle remaining 1 cup of cheese on top and bake just until cheese melts, 3-5 minutes. Serves 7.

*Better than Bouillon™ is the bouillon paste recommended. If using bouillon cubes reduce or eliminate the salt as bouillon cubes contain more salt than the bouillon paste.

# Savory Lentil Loaf with Mushroom Gravy

## Lentil Loaf:
**2 Tbsp. butter**
**1 large onion, finely chopped**
**2 stalks celery, finely chopped**
**2 large cloves garlic, minced**
**1 4-oz. can mushrooms, drained**
 **& finely chopped, opt.**
**2 cups cooked lentils**
**½ cup walnuts, finely chopped**
**½ cup pecans, finely chopped**
**½ cup oat bran**
**1 cup shredded sharp cheddar cheese**
**2 eggs, beaten**
**1½ tsp. Vege-Sal® or seasoning salt**
**½ tsp. black pepper**
**¾ tsp. poultry seasoning**
**1 tsp. soy liquid aminos or soy sauce**

## Mushroom Gravy:
**1 10.5-oz. can cream of mushroom soup, undiluted**
**⅓-½ cup water**
**1 tsp. beef bouillon paste or 1 cube beef bouillon***

Heat butter in a large non-stick skillet. Add onion, celery, garlic, and mushrooms and sauté until vegetables are tender. Place vegetable mixture into a bowl. Add lentils, nuts, and oat bran. Mix well. Add remaining loaf ingredients. Mix well. Line a regular-sized loaf pan with parchment paper, on bottom and sides. Trim excess paper away. Spoon lentil mixture into lined pan. Press down and into corners and smooth top with spoon or spatula. Cover top with foil and seal around edges of loaf pan. Place pan in a large roaster with cover. Carefully pour enough boiling water into roaster so the water comes just over half way up the side of the loaf pan. Be careful to pour water along side of loaf pan, not over the top. Place the roaster cover on top of roaster. Place into preheated oven and bake at 275° for 2 hours or until loaf is firm to the touch. Remove loaf pan from roaster and let cool for 15 minutes. Turn out lentil loaf onto a serving platter. To make gravy: whisk gravy ingredients together in a saucepan. Heat to boiling, stirring occasionally. Slice lentil loaf as you would a meat loaf. Ladle gravy over each slice. Serves 8.

Note: to reheat, bake slices on an oil-sprayed baking sheet at 350° for 10 minutes, or fry slices in butter in a non-stick skillet. Drizzle with warmed gravy.

Variation: use all walnuts, all pecans, or try hazelnuts, cashews, or almonds. Nuts can be finely chopped or ground into a meal.

*Better than Bouillon™ is the bouillon paste recommended. If using bouillon cubes loaf will be saltier.

## Pizza Burger Bean Loaf

1 15-oz. can black beans,
   rinsed & drained
1 14.5-oz. can diced tomatoes, drained
1 small onion, chopped
1 lb. ground beef
2 eggs
⅓ cup oat bran
¾ tsp. Italian seasoning
1 tsp. garlic powder
¾ tsp. salt
1 cup cubed or diced mozzarella,
   provolone, or Monterey Jack cheese

Place beans, tomatoes, and onion into a food processor and pulse to coarsely chop. Pour into a bowl. Add ground beef and mix well. Add remaining ingredients and mix well. Pour into an oil-sprayed loaf pan. Press into place with a spatula and smooth top. Bake at 375º for 1 hour and 30 minutes. Slice into thick slices and serve with warm spaghetti sauce or pizza sauce ladled over slices. Serves 6-8.

Variations: make ahead of time, chill, slice and fry in butter until crisp on both sides, and serve with sauce. For **Pizza Burger Bean Loaf Parmigiana,** place slices in an oil-sprayed baking pan, cover with hot spaghetti sauce and cheese, cover and bake at 350º for 20-30 minutes, until cheese has melted.

Vegetables you will encounter in these pages may be new or used in different ways than you've seen them before. Below are pictured some of the more obscure varieties for your grocery shopping-convenience.

Clockwise from top left: leek, spaghetti squash, kale, eggplant, green onion. On right, moving downward: butternut squash, red onion, chives, daikon. Center, right to left: radishes, onion and shallot, yellow squash. Middle left, to left: parsnip, green beans, yellow wax beans, turnip, jicama.

# Vegetables & Side Dishes

## Awesome Refried Beans

4 cups dry pinto beans
3 tsp. baking soda, divided
1 lb. turkey bacon, diced
3 Tbsp. olive oil
1 large onion, chopped
1 4-oz. can mild diced chilies

Soak beans overnight or use the a quick soaking method found on **page 13**. Drain. Place beans in a large pot and cover with water about 2" over beans. Add 1 tsp. baking soda. Bring to a boil until foaming. Pour off water and rinse beans in a colander. Place back in pot and add same amount of water and baking soda. Bring to a boil until foaming. Pour off water and rinse again. Place back in pot for the third time, add one tsp. baking soda. Bring to a boil until foaming. Drain water off and rinse beans. Return to pot and cover with water again, but do not add baking soda. Cook on low heat until beans start to mush. Stir frequently and add a little water if beans seem to be getting too dry. Be careful not to scorch beans in the bottom of the pot. When beans are tender, mash them with a potato masher. Heat olive oil in a large non-stick skillet. Add diced bacon and fry until crisp. Scoop out bacon with a slotted spoon and set aside. Fry onions in drippings until tender, adding a little oil if necessary. Add green chilies and mix together with onions. Mix onion and chili mixture into beans. Continue to cook beans until soft and mushy. Stir in bacon. This makes a very large batch, 8 cups.

Note: The refried beans freeze well. Place in either 1-2 cup freezer containers or zipper-style freezer bags.

## Delicious Refried Beans

2 slices turkey bacon, diced
2 Tbsp. olive oil
⅓ cup diced onion
1 Tbsp. canned diced green chilies
¼ cup salsa
1 16-oz. can refried beans

Fry bacon in hot olive oil until crisp. Remove with a slotted spoon and set aside. Add onions to drippings and sauté until tender. Add chilies, salsa, refried beans and bacon to pan. Heat through. Use in any recipe that calls for refried beans. Pictured at right with topping for **Delicious Refried Bean Salad (page 59)**. Serves 3.

**150**

## Cowboy Beans

5 cups water, divided
1 medium onion, quartered
3 large cloves garlic
1 large carrot, peeled & cut into chunks
2 cups dry pinto beans, sorted & washed
¼ tsp. cayenne pepper
½ tsp. ginger
1 tsp. chili powder or taco seasoning
1-1½ tsp. salt
1 cup salsa, reserved

Place 1 cup water, onion, garlic and carrot in a blender. Pulse until vegetables are finely chopped. Place chopped vegetables, remaining water and beans into a slow cooker. Cook on high for 8 hours. Add seasonings and salt. Cook on low for another 8 hours. Mash slightly and add salsa. To bake in oven, place all ingredients, except salsa, into a 5-6 quart pot. Cover and cook overnight at 200° for about 12 hours. Add salsa after beans are cooked to desired doneness and mashed. Makes 6-8 cups.

Variation: **Cowboy Beef & Beans:** when adding salsa stir in 1 lb. ground beef that has been cooked, drained, and seasoned with taco seasoning. Simmer 15-20 minutes. Freezes well.

## Hot & Spicy Mexican Beans

2 Tbsp. olive oil
1 large onion, quartered & sliced
2 cloves garlic, minced
1 large green pepper, quartered
    & julienned
1 large jalapeño pepper, minced
2 tsp. chili powder
½ tsp. salt
1 14.5-oz. can diced tomatoes
1 14.5-oz. can diced tomatoes
    with green chilies
1 19-oz. can cannellini beans,
    rinsed & drained

Heat oil in a large non-stick skillet or Dutch oven with a tight fitting lid. Add onions and garlic and sauté for 3 minutes, stirring frequently. Add green pepper, jalapeño pepper, chili powder, and salt. Cook for 1 minute. Stir in tomatoes and beans and bring to a boil. Cover, reduce heat, and simmer for 30 minutes. These have a real kick to them, so not for the faint of heart. Serve with a dollop of sour cream. Serves 6-8.

## El Rancho Beans

1 28-oz. can baked beans, rinsed & drained
1 16-oz can kidney beans,
    rinsed & drained
½ lb. ground beef, browned & drained
½ cup ketchup
½ cup onion, chopped
½ lb. turkey bacon, diced
    & fried crisp
1 Tbsp. vinegar
1 tsp. salt
2 Tbsp. Worcestershire sauce
2 tsp. dry mustard

Mix all ingredients together. For slow cooker, heat on stovetop then place in slow cooker for 2 hours on high. For oven, place in covered baking dish and bake at 350º for 40 minutes. Serves 8-10.

Variation: Replace kidney beans with two 15-oz. cans of black beans, rinsed and drained.

## Saucy Beans & Rice

1 Tbsp. olive oil
1 large clove garlic, minced
1 15.5-oz. can black-eyed peas,
    rinsed & drained
1 15.5-oz. can Great Northern beans,
    rinsed & drained
1½ cups frozen cauliflower, thawed
½ cup sour cream
½ cup water
2 tsp. chicken bouillon paste or 2 cubes chicken bouillon*
1 egg, beaten

Heat oil in a large non-stick skillet. Sauté garlic for a few minutes over medium heat. Do not brown or garlic will become bitter. Add beans and stir. Place cauliflower in food processor and pulse a few times until cauliflower resembles rice (cauli-rice). Pour cauli-rice in pan with beans. Toss gently until mixture is hot. In a small bowl whisk together sour cream, water, and bouillon. Pour into bean mixture and heat. Quickly whisk in egg. Stir and continue cooking for several minutes, until sauce has thickened slightly. Do not allow to boil. Remove from heat and serve. Serves 6.

*Better than Bouillon™ is the bouillon paste recommended. If using bouillon cubes recipe will be saltier.

## Garden Burritos

1 Tbsp. olive oil
2 medium carrots, shredded
2 small zucchini, shredded
½ cup minced onion
1 medium red or yellow sweet pepper, diced
1 15-oz. can black beans, rinsed & drained
1 15-oz. can red beans, rinsed & drained
¾ cup chipotle or medium salsa
2 Tbsp. taco seasoning
2 tsp. cumin, opt.
1 cup shredded mozzarella cheese
Chickpea Tortillas (page 175)

Heat oil in a large non-stick skillet. Sauté carrots, zucchini, onion, and sweet pepper over medium heat for 3-5 minutes, until tender. Add beans, salsa, taco seasoning, and cumin (if using). Heat for 5-7 minutes, until hot. Remove from heat and stir in cheese. Spoon into tortillas. Serves 4-6.

## Three Bean Au Gratin

1 lb. package frozen baby mixed beans
   & carrots
2 Tbsp. butter
2 Tbsp. garbanzo bean flour
1¼ cups Almond Milk (page 107)
¼ tsp. black pepper
¼ tsp. Worcestershire sauce
1 16-oz. can baby lima or butter beans,
   rinsed & drained
½ cup grated Parmesan cheese

Prepare baby mixed beans & carrots according to package directions. Drain and set aside. In a large saucepan, heat butter. Whisk in flour. Add milk and bring to a boil, stirring constantly. Add pepper and Worcestershire sauce. Mix in lima or butter beans and green bean mix. Pour bean mixture into an oil-sprayed 1½ quart casserole dish. Sprinkle top with Parmesan cheese. Bake uncovered at 350° for 30 minutes or until hot and bubbly. Serves 4.

## German Lima Beans

3 slices turkey bacon, diced
2 Tbsp. olive oil
¼ cup diced red onion
1 15-oz. can baby butter or baby
    lima beans, rinsed & drained
2 tsp. apple cider vinegar
1 Tbsp. seasoned rice vinegar
½ tsp. salt
¼ tsp. black pepper

In a non-stick skillet, fry diced bacon in oil until crisp. Remove bacon with a slotted spoon and set aside. Add onion to drippings and fry until tender. Place apple cider vinegar and ¼ cup beans in a food processor and puree until smooth. Scrape mixture into onions. Add remaining whole beans, seasoned rice vinegar, salt, pepper, and bacon. Stir and continue cooking until hot. Allow to cool to lukewarm before serving. This recipe is similar to German potato salad. Serves 2-3.

## Stewed Limas

1 Tbsp. butter
2 Tbsp. diced onion
1 14.5-oz. can diced tomatoes
1 15-oz. can lima or baby butter beans,
    rinsed & drained
¼ tsp. salt
¼ tsp. garlic powder
¾ tsp. chili powder
1½ Tbsp. garbanzo bean flour
2 Tbsp. water
1 cup shredded sharp cheddar cheese,
    divided

In a medium saucepan, sauté onion in butter. Add tomatoes, beans, salt, garlic powder, chili powder, garbanzo flour, and water. Mix well. Cook over low heat until mixture thickens. Spray a casserole dish with oil and spread ½ of the bean mixture into the bottom. Sprinkle ½ cup cheese over bean mixture. Spread remaining bean mixture over cheese. Bake at 350° for 20 minutes. Sprinkle with remaining cheese and continue baking 3-4 minutes, until cheese melts. Serves 3.

Variation: layer bean mixture and cheese in individual ramekins and bake as above.

## Sage Lima Beans

1 15-oz. can green lima beans,
   rinsed & drained
½ cup water
½ tsp. chicken bouillon paste or ½ cube chicken
   bouillon*
1 small bay leaf
½ tsp. sage
⅛ tsp. black pepper

Combine all ingredients in a small saucepan. Bring to
a boil. Reduce heat and simmer uncovered for 10 minutes. Stir occasionally. Remove bay leaf.

Variation: sauté ½-1 cup chopped onion until tender and add to saucepan before cooking.

*Better than Bouillon™ is the bouillon paste recommended. If using bouillon cubes recipe will be saltier.

## Parmesan Lima Beans

4 slices turkey bacon, diced
2 Tbsp. olive oil
2 cloves garlic, minced
⅛ tsp. oregano
2 Tbsp. water
1 15-oz. can green lima beans,
   rinsed & drained
¼ tsp. salt, opt.
¼ cup grated Parmesan cheese

In a medium skillet, cook bacon in hot oil until crisp. Remove bacon with a slotted spoon and set aside. Sauté garlic in drippings for 2 minutes over medium heat. Add oregano, water, beans, and salt. Stir and continue cooking until hot. Add Parmesan cheese and bacon, and cook 2 minutes longer. Serves 2-3.

## Lemon Pepper Limas & Carrots

1 Tbsp. butter
1 medium onion, diced
1 15-oz. can green lima beans,
    rinsed & drained
1 14.5-oz. can sliced carrots, drained
    or 1 cup frozen sliced carrots, thawed
¼ cup Almond Milk (page 107)
½ tsp. lemon pepper

Heat butter in a medium skillet. Sauté onion until tender. Add lima beans and carrots. Cook until vegetables are hot. Stir in almond milk and lemon pepper. Heat through. Serves 5-6.

## Lima Beans in Alfredo Sauce

2-4 Tbsp. butter
3 Tbsp. minced onion
3 Tbsp. minced green pepper
¼ cup cream cheese
¼ cup Almond Milk (page 107)
⅓ cup Parmesan cheese
1 15-oz. can baby lima or butter beans,
    rinsed & drained

Heat butter in a saucepan, using larger amount if a buttery sauce is desired. Add onion and green pepper. Sauté 3 minutes, or until vegetables are tender-crisp. Add cream cheese and stir until melted. Add almond milk and Parmesan cheese. Stir until well blended. Add beans and heat through. Serves 3.

Variation: add ¼ cup diced zucchini and sauté with the onion and green pepper.

## Baked Lima Bean Pudding

2 15-oz. cans lima or butter beans,
    rinsed & drained
1 cup Almond Milk (page 107)
¼ cup chopped onion
3 Tbsp. butter
2 Tbsp. garbanzo bean flour
½ tsp. salt
½ tsp. black pepper
½ tsp. garlic powder
2 eggs, beaten

Place beans into a food processor and puree until smooth. Set aside. Puree almond milk and onion in a blender. Set aside. Heat butter in a large saucepan. Whisk in garbanzo bean flour. Whisk in almond-onion milk, salt, pepper, and garlic powder. Whisk while cooking until mixture comes to a boil. Boil for 1 minute. Stir beans into milk mixture. Stir in beaten eggs. Pour into an oil-sprayed 8x8" casserole dish. Bake at 350º 45-55 minutes, until a knife inserted into the middle comes out clean. Serve with butter or your favorite potato topping. Serves 6-8.

## Zesty Butter Beans

2 Tbsp. onion, chopped
2 Tbsp. green pepper, chopped
1 Tbsp. butter
1 10.75-oz. can tomato soup, condensed
¼ cup water
1 Tbsp. apple cider vinegar
1 tsp. yellow prepared mustard
2 16-oz. cans butter beans, rinsed & drained

In skillet, brown onion and green pepper in butter. Add tomato soup, water, vinegar, and mustard. Heat. Place beans in buttered 8x8" glass baking dish. Pour sauce evenly over beans. Bake uncovered at 375º for 45 minutes. Garnish with shredded cheese. Serves 4-6.

**157**

## Creamy Navy Beans

1 Tbsp. butter
3 green onion tops & bottoms, sliced
1 Tbsp. garbanzo bean flour
¼ tsp. salt
½ cup Almond Milk (page 107)
2 Tbsp. sour cream
2 Tbsp. salad dressing (i.e. Thousand Island,
   Ranch, or Caesar dressing)
1 19-oz. can navy beans,
   rinsed & drained

In a small saucepan, sauté onion in butter until tender. Stir in garbanzo flour and salt. Whisk in almond milk. Cook, stirring constantly, until mixture thickens and becomes bubbly. Whisk in sour cream and dressing. Add beans and stir. Heat through but do not boil. Serves 3-5.

## Jamaican Red Beans

1 Tbsp. olive oil
1 medium onion, chopped
1 stalk celery, chopped
¾ cup water
1 tsp. vegetable bouillon paste or 1 cube vegetable bouillon*
1 15.5-oz. can red beans,
   rinsed & drained
1 medium bay leaf
½ tsp. dried leaf thyme
¼ tsp. crushed red pepper flakes
⅛ tsp. allspice

Heat oil in a medium saucepan. Sauté onion and celery until tender. Add remaining ingredients and stir. Bring to a boil. Reduce heat and simmer uncovered for 10-12 minutes. Remove bay leaf. Serves 6.

*Better than Bouillon™ is the bouillon paste recommended. If using bouillon cubes recipe will be saltier.

## Leeks, Beans, and Bacon

¼ cup olive oil
6 slices turkey bacon, diced
2-3 leeks, white & tender green parts, sliced
1 15-oz. can kidney beans, rinsed & drained
Salt to taste
Black pepper to taste

Heat oil in a large skillet. Add bacon and fry until crisp. Remove bacon with a slotted spoon and set aside. Add leeks to pan and sauté for 10 minutes. Add beans and bacon. Stir well. Cook until beans are hot. Salt and pepper to taste. Serves 6-8.

## Mushroom Lentil Casserole

¾ cup dried lentils, sorted & rinsed
2¼ cups water, divided
3 tsp. vegetable bouillon paste or 3 cubes
    vegetable bouillon*
16-oz. frozen cauliflower, thawed
⅔ cup chopped onion
⅔ cup chopped celery
1 4-oz. can mushroom stems & pieces,
    drained & chopped
¼ cup coarsely chopped walnuts
1-1½ tsp. Vege Sal® or seasoning salt,
    to taste
½ tsp. thyme
¼ cup + 2 Tbsp. grated Parmesan cheese,
    divided

Place lentils, 2 cups water, and 2 tsp. bouillon into a saucepan. Bring to a boil. Reduce heat and simmer for 25 minutes. Meanwhile, place cauliflower into a food processor and pulse until it resembles rice. Transfer to a bowl and mix in ¼ cup water and remaining 1 tsp. bouillon. Set aside. In a large bowl combine remaining ingredients, except 2 Tbsp. cheese. Drain lentils if necessary. Mix in lentils and cauliflower. Spread into an oil-sprayed 9x13" casserole dish. Sprinkle with 2 Tbsp. Parmesan cheese. Cover and bake at 350º for 35-45 minutes, until hot. Vegetables should be tender-crisp. Uncover and bake 5 minutes longer to lightly brown top. Serves 9.

*Better than Bouillon™ is the bouillon paste recommended. If using bouillon cubes reduce or eliminate the salt as bouillon cubes contain more salt than the bouillon paste.

## Broiled Cannellini Tomatoes

3 medium tomatoes
1-1¼ cups Horseradish Cream Bean Dip (page 47)
    or Basil Pesto Spread (page 38)
2 cups shredded cheddar or mozzarella cheese

Cut both ends off tomatoes and discard ends.  Slice tomatoes into thick slices, about 4 slices per tomato.  Lay slices on a broiler pan and spread each with dip or spread.  Sprinkle with cheese.  Broil 4 inches from heat for 3-4 minutes or just until cheese is melted.  Cheddar cheese works best if using **Horseradish Cream Bean Dip**, and mozzarella works best if using **Basil Pesto Spread**.  Makes 12-14 slices.

## Cannellini & Tomato Bake

½ cup hot water
1 tsp. beef bouillon paste or 1 cube beef bouillon*
6 Tbsp. grated Parmesan cheese
1 Tbsp. chopped fresh parsley
1 tsp. dried basil
1 tsp. dried chives
1 19-oz. can cannellini beans,
    rinsed & drained
1 large onion, halved and thinly sliced
3 medium tomatoes, peeled & sliced

Stir bouillon into hot water and set aside.  In a small bowl, combine cheese, parsley, basil, and chives.  Set aside.  Spray with oil an 8" casserole dish.  Layer ½ of the beans in bottom of dish, then ½ of the onions, ½ of the tomatoes, and ½ of the cheese mixture.  Layer remaining beans, onions, and tomatoes.  Pour bouillon mixture over top of all layers.  Sprinkle remaining cheese mixture over top of layers.  Cover and bake at 350° for 45 minutes.  Uncover and bake 15 minutes longer, or until top is golden brown.  Serves 6-8.

*Better than Bouillon™ is the bouillon paste recommended.  If using bouillon cubes recipe will be saltier.

## Cannellini Rarebit

2 Tbsp. butter
¼ cup chopped sweet onion
½ cup chopped green pepper
2 15-oz. cans cannellini beans,
    rinsed & drained
2 Tbsp. ketchup
1 tsp. Worcestershire sauce
¼ tsp. salt, opt.
⅛ tsp. black pepper
8-oz. cheddar cheese, shredded

Heat butter in a large non-stick skillet. Sauté onion and green pepper until tender-crisp. Stir in remaining ingredients, except cheese. In an oil-sprayed 1 quart casserole dish, layer ½ of bean mixture, ½ of cheese, remaining bean mixture, and remaining cheese. Cover and bake at 350º for 30-35 minutes, until hot and cheese has melted. Serves 6.

Variation: replace cannellini beans with red kidney beans.

## Cauliflower Curry

1 Tbsp. olive oil
1 large clove garlic, minced
1 tsp. curry powder
1 tsp. ginger
1 tsp. salt
¼ tsp. cardamom
1 head cauliflower,
    cut into bite-sized florets
1 small unpeeled zucchini,
    washed & diced
1 15.5-oz. can garbanzo beans,
    rinsed & drained
½ cup water
10-oz. frozen peas, thawed

Heat oil in a large non-stick skillet. Stir in garlic, curry powder, ginger, salt, and cardamom. Stir and cook over low heat for 2 minutes. Add cauliflower, zucchini, garbanzo beans, and water. Stir well and bring just to a boil. Reduce heat, cover, and simmer 10-15 minutes, until almost tender. Add peas and continue to simmer for 5 minutes, or until vegetables are tender. Serves 8.

## Smothered Lentils

1 lb. (2 cups) dried lentils, rinsed & sorted
1 medium onion, chopped
2 large cloves garlic, minced
2 stalks celery, chopped
1 cup baby carrots, chopped
1 cup tomatoes, diced
1 heaping cup of meat
    from smoked turkey legs
1 tsp. marjoram
1 tsp. ground coriander
1 tsp. salt
¼-½ tsp. hickory smoke salt, to taste
½ tsp. black pepper
4 cups water

Combine all ingredients in a slow cooker.  Cover and cook on low 6-7 hours.  Serves 8.

Variation:  replace smoked turkey leg meat with cooked ham or turkey ham.

Note:  Hickory Smoke salt is found in the spice section of your grocery store.

## Four Bean Hotdish

1 15-oz. can kidney beans,
    rinsed & drained
1 15-oz. can pinto beans,
    rinsed & drained
1 16-oz. can baked beans,
    rinsed, drained, & divided
1 14.5-oz. can French style green beans,
    drained
1 medium green pepper, diced
1 bunch green onion, tops & bottoms,
    sliced
1 cup ketchup
1 tsp. chili powder

Place kidney and pinto beans into a 2 quart casserole dish.  Reserve ½ cup baked beans and pour remaining baked beans into dish with kidney and pinto beans.  Add green beans, green pepper, and green onions.  Place the ½ cup reserved baked beans into a food processor.  Add ketchup and chili powder.  Puree until smooth.  Add ¼ cup ketchup puree to the bean mixture.  Stir well.  Spread remaining ketchup mixture over top of casserole.  Bake uncovered at 350° for 1 hour, or until heated through and bubbly.  Serves 8-10.

## Sautéed Butternut Squash with Black Beans

1 Tbsp. olive oil
1 small onion, diced
1 small butternut squash, seeded,
    peeled, and cut into ½" cubes
¼ tsp. garlic powder
½ tsp. salt
¼ cup red wine vinegar
¼ cup water
2 15-oz. cans black beans,
    rinsed & drained
½ tsp. oregano

Heat oil in a large non-stick skillet (with a lid) or Dutch oven.  Add onion, squash, garlic powder, and salt.  Sauté over medium heat for 5 minutes, or until onion is tender.  Add vinegar and water.  Cover and cook for 10 minutes, or until squash is tender.  Add beans and oregano.  Heat through.  Serves 6.

## Pumpkin Pie

1 bean flour pie crust (page 180)
2 eggs
1 15-oz. can (2 cups) pumpkin
½ tsp. salt
1½ tsp. allspice
½ tsp. ginger or nutmeg
½ tsp. cloves
1⅔ cups evaporated milk
    or light cream

Prepare pie crust.  Beat eggs with a mixer and add remaining ingredients.  Pour into pie crust.  Bake at 425° for 15 minutes.  Reduce heat to 350° and bake 20-30 minutes longer, until knife inserted in center comes out clean.  Cool before serving.  Makes 1 pie and serves 6-8.

If desired, top with unsweetened whipped cream.

## Crockpot Spaghetti Squash (pasta substitute)

**1 small or medium spaghetti squash**

Cut spaghetti squash in half lengthwise and scoop out seeds and membranes. Place halves back together and set in slow cooker. Make sure to purchase a squash that fits slow cooker. Do not add any liquid. Cover and cook on low for 5-7 hours for small squash and up to 8 hours for a larger one. To check for doneness, squash will give when gently pressed. Pull spaghetti strands out with a fork, pulling from around the middle, not lengthwise. They will pull out easily if squash is fully cooked. Place strands in casserole dish. Use to replace pasta in other recipes. Seeds can be reserved to make **Baked Pumpkin Seeds (page 24)**.

## Microwave Spaghetti Squash (pasta substitute)

**1 small or medium spaghetti squash**

Microwave squash for one minute. Remove from microwave and cut lengthwise. Remove seeds and membranes. Place cut side down in ¼ to ½ cup water. Microwave for approximately 12 minutes or until tender. Pull spaghetti strands out with a fork, pulling from around the middle, not lengthwise.

## Parmesan Spaghetti Squash (pasta substitute)

**1 medium spaghetti squash (about 4 lbs.)**
**½ tsp. garlic salt or powder**
**¼ tsp. lemon pepper**
**2-3 Tbsp. butter, sliced**
**¼ cup grated Parmesan cheese**

Cut the squash lengthwise and remove seeds and membrane. Put halves back together and place on a baking sheet. Bake at 400° for 45-60 minutes. To check for doneness, squash will give when gently pressed. Let cool slightly. Fork out strands and place in casserole dish. Add remaining ingredients and toss gently while still hot to melt butter.
Serves 6-8.

## Stuffed Spaghetti Squash (pasta substitute)

1 medium spaghetti squash
1 Tbsp. olive oil
1 medium onion, chopped
1 cup zucchini or yellow squash,
   unpeeled, diced
1 medium tomato, diced
1 cup cooked lentils
1 cup spaghetti sauce,
   with or without meat

### Toppings:
Butter
Grated Parmesan cheese

Cut spaghetti squash in half lengthwise. Scoop seeds and membranes out with a spoon, being careful not to scoop out flesh or meat of squash. Discard seeds and membranes. Lay squash halves face up onto a baking sheet. Set aside. Heat oil in a large non-stick skillet. Add onion and zucchini and sauté until onions are tender. Add tomatoes, lentils, and spaghetti sauce. Cook until mixture is hot. Spoon stuffing into each half. Cover halves and baking sheet with aluminum foil. Bake at 350° for 2 hours or until squash gives easily when shell is pressed. With a fork, loosen squash. Loosen strands by pulling from the sides and toward the middle. Work your way from the center to the ends. Scoop out loosened spaghetti squash and stuffing with a spoon, dividing strands. Place into a serving bowl. Top individual servings with a dollop of butter and sprinkle with Parmesan cheese. Serves 8-10.

## Cabbage Noodles (pasta substitute)

½ head cabbage
¼ cup butter
¼-½ tsp. lemon pepper
½ tsp. Vege-Sal® or seasoning salt

Slice cabbage into ¼″ strips so they resemble fettuccini noodles. Separate the pieces so they are not in clumps. Place cabbage into a covered pot in a couple of inches of water. Cook 8 minutes, or until tender. Cabbage must be soft to achieve noodle feel. Drain cabbage thoroughly. Toss cabbage noodles with butter, lemon pepper and Vege Sal®. Eat plain or cover with alfredo, stroganoff, spaghetti, or other sauce. Serves 6.

## Mock Mashed Potatoes (potato substitute)

1 cup yellow split peas
1½ cups water
1 Tbsp. bouillon paste or 3 cubes bouillon,
   chicken or beef*
1 medium bay leaf
½ tsp. sage
1 Tbsp. extra virgin olive oil
1 large clove garlic, minced
½ medium sweet onion, chopped
¼ cup butter
½ tsp. black pepper

Rinse split peas in a colander.  Place into a bowl and cover with 2½ cups water.  Let soak for 8 hours.  Do not over soak.  Drain in colander.  Mix together 1½ cups water and bouillon in a pan.  Add peas.  Bring just to a boil.  Skim off foam that rises to the surface.  Reduce heat to a simmer.  Add bay leaf and sage.  Simmer for 15 minutes or until peas are tender.  Do not overcook or mixture will have a pudding consistency instead of mashed potato consistency.  Immediately drain peas over a bowl to reserve broth.  Add a little broth after pureeing, if necessary.  Remove bay leaf.  In a sauté pan heat olive oil and sauté onion and garlic on medium-low heat until onions are soft, about 5 minutes.  Place peas, onion and garlic, butter, and pepper into a food processor.  Puree until smooth.  Serve with butter or gravy.  Serves 6.
Variation:   replace yellow split peas with cannellini beans.  Soak overnight, drain and rinse.  Cover with water and bouillon and boil until tender, 45-60 minutes.
*Better than Bouillon™ is the bouillon paste recommended.  If using bouillon cubes recipe will be saltier.

## Quick Mock Mashed Potatoes (potato substitute)

1 15-oz. can cannellini beans,
   rinsed & well drained
1 tsp. bouillon paste or 1 cube bouillon,
   chicken or beef*
¼ tsp. sage
¼ tsp. black pepper
2 Tbsp. butter
½ small onion, chopped
1 small clove garlic, chopped
1 small bay leaf

Place beans, bouillon, sage, and pepper into a food processor.  Sauté onion, garlic, and bay leaf in butter until onions are tender, 5-7 minutes.  Do not brown vegetables or the garlic will turn bitter.  Discard bay leaf.  Scrape onion mixture with any excess butter into food processor. Process until smooth.  Heat "mock" potatoes in a pan or in microwave until hot.  Serves 2.
Variation:  use 19-oz. can of beans in place of 15-oz. can.  Other kinds of beans will work as well.
*Better than Bouillon™ is the bouillon paste recommended.  If using bouillon cubes recipe will be saltier.

**166**

## Cheesy Turnip 'Tatoes (potato substitute)

3 medium turnips, peeled and cubed
  (3½-4 cups)
1 15-oz. can cannellini beans,
  rinsed & drained
3 Tbsp. butter
¼-½ tsp. salt, to taste
¼-½ tsp. garlic powder
  (sage, oregano or taco seasoning)
4-oz. cheddar cheese, shredded

Place cubed turnips into an 8x8" glass baking dish. Add 2 Tbsp. water and cover with plastic wrap. Microwave for 13 minutes, or until very tender, stirring occasionally. Stir in beans and microwave for 2 minutes. Remove from microwave and drain. Place turnip mixture into a food processor and add remaining ingredients, except cheese. Puree until smooth. Place mixture back into baking dish and add cheese. Microwave for 3 minutes, or until cheese melts and turnips are hot and creamy. Parsnips can be used in place of turnips. Serves 4-6.

Variation: make **Mexican 'Tatoes** by adding 2 Tbsp. salsa, shredded cheddar cheese and a dollop of sour cream on top of each serving.

## Daikon "French Fries" (potato substitute)

1 large Daikon radish

### Seasoning:
½ tsp. paprika
½ tsp. garlic powder
½ tsp. fresh ground pepper
1/8 tsp. cayenne pepper
1 tsp. salt
3 Tbsp. extra virgin olive oil

Peel a Daikon radish and cut it into French fries. Fries will shrink slightly in oven, so do not cut too thin. Spread fries evenly on a large baking sheet. Sprinkle oil over fries and toss. In a small bowl combine seasonings. Sprinkle seasonings over fries and toss well. Spread in a single layer. Bake at 425° for 40 minutes, or until very brown. Turn every 10 minutes while cooking. Serve immediately. Serves 1-2.

Variation: Replace Daikon radish with any root vegetable—rutabaga, parsnips, turnips, celery root or sweet potato.

## Parsnip Gnocchi with Thyme Butter (pasta substitute)

### Gnocchi:
1 lb. parsnips, peeled
1¾ cups garbanzo bean flour
1 egg
1 tsp. salt
½ tsp. black pepper
1 tsp. onion powder
2 Tbsp. grated Parmesan cheese

### Thyme Butter:
½ cup butter
4 tsp. fresh thyme or 1½ tsp. dried thyme

Boil parsnips for 15 minutes, or until tender when pierced with a fork. Drain and mash parsnips. Add remaining dumpling ingredients. Knead several times forming a soft dough. Knead in extra bean flour if necessary. Cut dough into portions. On a board dusted with bean flour, roll each piece into a long rope, similar to a pencil. Cut into 3/4" pieces. Slightly press each piece with a lightly floured fork. Bring 4 quarts of water to a boil and add 1 tsp. salt. Quickly drop gnocchi, one by one, into the pot. Cook in batches. Stir water a couple of times with a wooden spoon to keep gnocchi from sticking together. In a few seconds gnocchi will rise to the surface of the water. Let cook for 1 minute on the surface, then remove with a slotted spoon. Keep warm. Continue cooking until all batches are done. In a large saucepan, melt butter over medium heat. Add thyme and stir. Add gnocchi and toss to gently coat. Serve hot. Makes 4 cups.

Note: these have a strong parsnip flavor. Replace parsnips with rutabagas or turnips for a milder flavor.

## Cauli-rice (rice substitute)

1 16-oz. bag frozen cauliflower, thawed
¼ cup hot water
1-2 Tbsp. bouillon paste or 3-6 cubes bouillon, beef or chicken*

Place cauliflower into a food processor and pulse until it resembles rice. This will not take long. Use short pulses and scrape down sides between pulses. (Plain cauli-rice can be used to replace rice in recipes). For flavored cauli-rice: place cauli-rice into a saucepan. Mix water and bouillon together and pour over cauli-rice. Heat and serve. Makes 2 cups. For cauli-couscous, pulse cauliflower longer until it resembles couscous.

*Better than Bouillon™ is the bouillon paste recommended. If using bouillon cubes recipe will be saltier.

## Grilled Swiss Veggie Pockets (potato substitute)

**3 slices of turkey bacon, diced & fried crisp**
**1 large jicama, peeled & thinly sliced**
**2 medium carrots, shredded**
**¼ cup leeks or green onion with tops**
**Vege Sal® or seasoning salt, to taste**
**¼ cup butter**
**1 cup shredded Swiss cheese**

Arrange jicama in 4 pieces of heavy foil for pockets. Divide carrots and onions and spread over foil pieces. Season with Vege Sal® or seasoning salt. Dot with butter. Fold foil loosely around veggies and crimp edges to seal. Place on grill for about 45 minutes, turning several times. Open pockets, add bacon and cheese and seal pockets again. Continue grilling until cheese has melted. Serves 8.

Variation: cook pockets in 400° oven for 45 minutes. Pockets do not need to be turned when baked in oven. Open pocket, add bacon and cheese, reseal and let stand until cheese melts.

## Roasted Italian Vegetables (potato substitute)

**2 medium red onions**
**4 large carrots**
**2 parsnips**

### Marinade:
**2 Tbsp. extra virgin olive oil**
**2 Tbsp. butter, melted**
**½ tsp. oregano**
**¼ tsp. garlic powder**
**¼ tsp. sweet basil**
**½ tsp. salt**
**¼ tsp. black pepper**

Peel onion and cut into wedges from top to root end so layers stay intact. Peel carrots and parsnips and cut into chunks. Steam carrots and parsnips for 10 minutes in a steamer, then transfer to a bowl. Mix together marinade and pour over vegetables. Toss gently. Spread in a single layer onto a foil lined 10x15" baking pan. Bake at 450° for 30-45 minutes or until caramelized, stirring occasionally. Serves 6-8.

# Breads & Rolls

## Bean Flour Yeast Bread

### 1 Regular Loaf:

1½ cups lukewarm water (100º)
1 package (2¼ tsp.) yeast
2¼ tsp. salt or seasoning salt
1 Tbsp. onion powder
1 tsp. xanthan gum (dough enhancer), opt.
1 heaping Tbsp. mayonnaise
1 egg
3-3½ cups garbanzo bean flour

### 2 Regular Loaves + 1 Small Loaf:

3 cups lukewarm water (100º)
2 packages (1½ Tbsp.) yeast
1½ Tbsp. salt or seasoning salt
2 Tbsp. onion powder
2 tsp. xanthan gum (dough enhancer), opt.
2 heaping Tbsp. mayonnaise
2 eggs
6-7 cups garbanzo bean flour

Whisk water, yeast, and salt together in a large bowl. Mix in onion powder, xanthan gum, mayonnaise, and egg. Add bean flour and whisk to mix. Dough should be the consistency of muffin batter. Cover bowl with waxed paper or something (not air-tight) just to keep dough from falling into bowl while it sits. Set timer for 2 hours if making 1 loaf, 2½ hours for larger batch. When time is up, the dough will be very sticky and fluffy. Dust with additional bean flour and cover again. Place in refrigerator and allow to sit for at least 1 hour. Dough will keep in refrigerator for up to 2 weeks.

To bake loaves: preheat oven to 350º and spray loaf pan or pans with oil. Let rise in warm place (stove top works well if oven is heating) until double or even with top of loaf pan, 30-60 minutes. Gently place pans in oven, being careful not to jar pans. If dough falls, let it rise again before baking. Bake for 30 minutes. Remove from pan onto a wire cooling rack. 1 regular loaf recipe will make 2 small loaves.

To bake pitas: preheat oven to 450º. Prepare baking stone or baking sheet by rubbing with a little olive oil. Measure out ½ cup of dough and place on a baking stone or baking sheet. Spread dough to ¼"-¾" thick. Bake for 8-10 minutes, until lightly browned. A toothpick inserted in pita should come out clean. A thin pita can be used as a wrap, a thicker pita can be split with a knife. 1 recipe makes 5-7 pitas.

To bake breadsticks: place dough into a zipper-style plastic bag. Cut off one corner and discard. Pipe 8-10 long breadsticks onto a prepared stone or oil-sprayed baking sheet. Dough can be made into different shapes such as 4 large **Pretzels**. Bake at 450º for 8-10 minutes, until browned on top.

Variation: add your favorite herbs or cheese to batter.
Note: if leaving out the xanthan gum, bread will be more crumbly.

## Garlic Toast

**1 batch, Bean Flour Yeast Bread  (page 171)**
**Butter**
**Garlic salt**

Prepare a regular batch of **Bean Flour Yeast Bread**, but place in 2 small oil-sprayed loaf pans.  Bake at 350º for 30 minutes.  Remove from pans and allow to cool on a rack.  Slice each loaf into ¼" slices.  Bread will slice better if cooled in refrigerator for a day.  Butter both sides of each slice and fry in skillet until browned on both sides.  Sprinkle lightly with garlic salt.  This will be a softer bread.  For drier garlic bread, place the buttered slices onto a cookie sheet and bake at 400º for 15 minutes, until browned on bottom.  Turn slices over and bake another 15 minutes.  Sprinkle lightly with garlic salt.  Makes about 48 slices.

## Bruschetta

**1 batch, regular loaf, Bean Flour Yeast Bread (page 171)**
**Extra virgin olive oil**

Prepare a regular batch of **Bean Flour Yeast Bread**, but bake in 2 small oil-sprayed loaf pans.  Bake at 350º for 30 minutes.  Remove from pans and allow to cool on a rack.  Slice each loaf into ¼" slices.  Bread will slice better if cooled in the refrigerator for a day.  Slices must be thin or bruschetta will not dry enough.  With a pastry brush, spread olive oil on both sides of each slice.  Place slices onto a baking sheet and bake at 400º for 15 minutes.  Turn slices over and bake another 10-15 minutes.  Bruschetta will be nicely browned on both sides, but not quite as crisp as bruschetta made with wheat flour.  These freeze well.  Thaw slices and re-crisp by baking at 400º for 10 minutes.  Makes about 48 slices.

## Note About Bean Flours

Bean flours are interchangeable.  White bean, black bean, red bean, and fava flours can all be used in place of garbanzo bean flour in any of these recipes.  Amounts may have to be adjusted slightly.  If you can find white bean flour, or mill your own, use it in place of garbanzo bean flour in any recipe.  It has a milder flavor than garbanzo bean flour.  Garbanzo bean flour was used in each of these recipes because it is easy to find in stores.

**172**

## Baking Powder Drop Biscuits

1½ cups white or garbanzo bean flour
½ cup oat bran
4 tsp. baking powder
1 tsp. cream of tartar
½ tsp. salt
3 Tbsp. extra virgin olive oil
⅔-¾ cup water

Mix bean flour, bran, baking powder, cream of tartar, and salt. Add oil and water and mix just until flour disappears. Immediately drop by spoonfuls onto an oil-sprayed baking sheet. Bake at 375º for 10-20 minutes (depending on size), until bottoms are golden brown. These biscuits do not rise very much. Makes 1 dozen.

Variation: for cheesy biscuits add 1 cup shredded sharp cheddar cheese to the dry ingredients; for added flavor, sauté 1 cup of onion and 2 cloves of garlic and add with the cheese.

## Note

Make up bean flour biscuits or tortillas to take with you when travel. Keep them in zipper-style storage bags. At fast food restaurants throw away the bun and replace it with one of these. Chicken tastes best on biscuits, burgers and roast beef are better on tortillas.

## Bean Flour Pancakes

½ cup garbanzo bean flour, sifted
¼ cup oat bran
¼-½ tsp. salt, to taste
1 tsp. baking powder
1½ Tbsp. safflower, walnut oil, or other light oil
½ cup water
1 egg

Combine dry ingredients in order given. Measure bean flour before sifting. Whisk in wet ingredients one at a time. Pour pancakes onto a hot, greased griddle or non-stick skillet. Turn pancakes when golden brown and brown other side. Makes approximately 10 small pancakes

Note: for a fluffier pancake, separate egg. Add yolk with the wet ingredients. Beat egg white and fold egg white into finished batter.

**173**

## Italian Breadsticks

### Dough:
**3-3¼ cups garbanzo bean flour**
**1 cup oat bran**
**2 Tbsp.+2 tsp. baking powder**
**2 tsp. cream of tartar**
**½ tsp. salt**
**2 tsp. Italian seasoning**
**⅓ cup safflower oil or light olive oil**
**1 cup water**

### Topping:
**2-3 Tbsp. butter, melted**
**¼-½ tsp. garlic powder**

Mix dry ingredients together in a bowl. Add oil and water and mix again. Let dough sit 5-10 minutes. Dough absorbs and thickens as it sits. Stir. Dough will be sticky. Add a little more flour if necessary. Spray a 9x13" glass baking pan with oil. Spread dough out into pan, greasing hands with butter and working the dough to spread evenly in pan. Cut dough into breadsticks using a pizza cutter or sharp knife. Bake at 400° for 25-30 minutes, until the sides and bottoms are lightly browned. Mix melted butter and garlic powder together and brush onto tops of breadsticks while still hot. Carefully re-cut and remove from pan. Dip breadsticks into hot pizza or spaghetti sauce. Breadsticks can be lightly dusted with Parmesan cheese while still in pan. Makes 14 breadsticks.

## Chickpea Individual Pizza Crusts

**1 cup garbanzo bean (chickpea) flour**
**½ tsp. salt**
**1 cup water**
**2 Tbsp. olive oil for frying**

Sift flour and salt into a bowl. Slowly add water, whisking constantly to form a batter. Beat with a wire whisk until smooth. Cover and let batter stand at room temperature for 30 minutes. Heat 1 Tbsp. olive oil in 10" non-stick skillet over medium-high heat. Stir batter and pour half (about ¾ cup) into skillet. Immediately swirl pan to evenly coat bottom of pan with batter. Cook until bottom is browned and top is set, about 2-3 minutes. Burst any air bubbles with the tip of a knife. Carefully loosen with a spatula and slide onto an oil-sprayed baking sheet or pizza pan. Heat another tablespoon of oil, stir batter, and cook second crust. These can be made up ahead of time. If necessary, blot tops before using. Makes 2 crusts.

Picture shown is **Chickpea Chicken Pizza (page 124)**.

## Chickpea Tortillas

2 cups garbanzo bean flour
2 tsp. onion powder
1 tsp. salt
1 tsp. baking soda
1 Tbsp. lemon juice
½ cup mayonnaise
    or unsweetened plain yogurt
2-2½ cups water
Butter for frying

Whisk together all ingredients, except butter. Batter will be the consistency of thin pancake batter. Heat 1-2 tsp. butter in a small non-stick skillet. Pour ¼ cup batter into pan. Immediately swirl pan around to coat bottom of pan with batter. Tiny holes in tortilla are fine. Fry over medium heat until brown on bottom and almost set on top, about 1 minute. Loosen edges and flip. Press slightly and fry until brown. Second side will not brown as evenly as first side. Remove and place on paper towel-lined plate. Add butter to pan before frying each tortilla. These will be the consistency of a crepe or thin pancake, and roll well. Makes 14 small tortillas.

## Cheesy Chili "Corn Bread"

1½ cups garbanzo bean flour
½ cup oat bran
4 tsp. baking powder
1 tsp. cream of tartar
¼ tsp. salt
1 tsp. garlic powder
1 tsp. onion powder
1 egg, beaten
1 4-oz. can mild diced chilies
½ cup water
3 Tbsp. safflower oil or light olive oil
1 cup shredded sharp cheddar cheese

Mix all ingredients together in a bowl. Pour into an oil-sprayed regular loaf pan. Bake at 400° for 35-40 minutes. This "Corn Bread" is best eaten hot out of the oven or toasted. Refrigerating allows the bread to slice better. Pop slices into a toaster and eat hot with butter or peanut butter. Makes 1 loaf.

## Broccoli Spoon Bread

1½ cups garbanzo bean flour
½ cup oat bran
4 tsp. baking powder
1 tsp. cream of tartar
½ tsp. salt
1 tsp. garlic powder
1 tsp. onion powder
5 eggs, beaten
1 14-oz. package frozen chopped broccoli,
   thawed & well drained
1½ cup shredded cheddar cheese
1½ cups small curd cottage cheese
1 medium onion, chopped
¾ cup butter, melted

In a large bowl, mix together bean flour, oat bran, baking powder, cream of tartar, salt, garlic powder, and onion powder. Add remaining ingredients and mix just until moistened. Spray a 9x13" cake pan with oil and spread mixture into pan. Bake uncovered at 350º for 40 minutes, or until a toothpick comes out clean. This can also be baked in 2 oil-sprayed loaf pans for 1 hour. If using bread pans, bread can be chilled, sliced, and fried to reheat. This is a very moist bread, similar to stuffing. Serve hot with butter. Serves 10.

## Vegetable Puffs

2 Tbsp. butter
2 cloves garlic, minced
1 medium onion, diced
4 carrots, peeled & shredded
2 10-oz. packages frozen chopped spinach,
   thawed & squeezed dry
4 eggs, beaten
¼ tsp. black pepper
2 Tbsp. chicken broth powder
¾ cup garbanzo bean flour

Heat butter in a small skillet. Sauté onion and garlic until tender. Set aside. In a large bowl combine carrots and spinach. Add eggs, pepper, chicken broth powder, flour, and onion mixture. Mix well. Spoon into oil-sprayed muffin tins, barely filling each muffin cup. Bake at 350º for 25 minutes, or until set and knife inserted in center comes out clean. Serve warm. Makes 18 puffs.

## Oat Bran Crackers

½ cup boiling water
1½ Tbsp. butter
1 cup oat bran
½ tsp. Vege Sal® or seasoning salt

Mix all ingredients together. Form dough into 18 balls, using a small trigger-style scoop. On a large, ungreased baking sheet, flatten each ball to the thickness of a soda cracker. Lightly sprinkle tops with additional seasoning salt, if desired. Bake at 350º for 20 minutes, or until very lightly browned on bottom. Store in refrigerator. Makes 18 crackers.

## Snack Sticks

½ cup oat bran
½ cup garbanzo bean flour
1½ tsp. baking powder
¼ tsp. salt
3 Tbsp. olive oil
1 egg
½ tsp. almond extract

### Seasoning Choices:
Sour cream and onion powder
Garlic powder and garlic salt
    (equal parts)
Powdered chicken broth
White cheddar cheese powder
Ranch dressing mix, dry

Combine snack sticks ingredients. Roll out to a ⅛" thick rectangle (about the thickness of a cracker) onto lightly bean-floured waxed paper, parchment paper, or silicone cutting mat. Place a large baking sheet on top of dough and carefully flip dough into the baking sheet. Score snack sticks with a pizza cutter. Bake at 350º for 15-20 minutes, until lightly browned on bottom. Use pizza cutter to separate sticks. Place seasoning of choice into a sandwich bag and gently shake a few sticks at a time to coat while still warm. Shake off excess seasoning. Makes 40 Snack Sticks.

Note: One recipe makes enough snack sticks to try many different seasonings.

**177**

## Fry Bread or Pita Crisps

½ cup oat bran
½ cup garbanzo bean flour
1½ tsp. baking powder
¼ tsp. salt
3 Tbsp. olive oil
1 egg
½ tsp. almond extract, optional
Oil for frying

Mix dough ingredients together. Lightly dust a cutting board or silicone cutting mat with bean flour. Roll out a tablespoon of dough at a time to about a 2 inch diameter. Fry Bread can be fried or baked. Makes 1 dozen.

To Fry: Heat oil, about 1" deep, in a cast iron skillet.
Oil is hot when standing a wooden spoon handle in pan,
bubbles form around handle. Reduce heat to medium-high. Place 2 Fry Breads in pan at a time. These will brown quickly. Turn when first side is lightly browned, frying ½-1 minute per side. Place Fry Bread (pictured) on a paper towel lined baking sheet. Continue to fry remaining pieces.
To Bake: Preheat oven to 350º. Bake on baking sheet 15-20 minutes or until lightly browned on bottoms.
For Pita Crisps: Cut each Fry Bread into 4 pie-shaped wedges with a pizza cutter. Lightly salt each wedge and bake as directed above.

## Rosemary Pita Crisps

½ cup oat bran
½ cup garbanzo bean flour
1 ½ tsp. baking powder
¼ tsp. salt
1 tsp. onion powder
1 tsp. dried crushed rosemary
3 Tbsp. olive oil
1 egg
**Seasoning:**
½ tsp. dried crushed rosemary
⅛-¼ tsp. salt
¼ tsp. garlic powder
¼ tsp. black pepper

Mix dough ingredients together. Lightly dust a cutting board or silicone cutting mat with bean flour. Roll out a tablespoon of dough at a time to about a 2 inch diameter. Mix seasoning together. Lightly sprinkle seasoning on top of each pita and spread with fingers to evenly disburse spices. Do not over salt. Slightly press seasoning into pita. Cut each pita into 4 pie-shaped wedges. Place wedges onto a baking sheet and bake at 350º for 10 minutes. Makes 40 crisps.

**178**

## Onion Dill Pita Crisps

½ cup oat bran
½ cup garbanzo bean flour
1½ tsp. baking powder
¼ tsp. salt
1 tsp. onion powder
1 tsp. dill weed
3 Tbsp. olive oil
1 egg

### Seasoning:
1 tsp. onion powder
1 tsp. dill weed
½ tsp. salt

Mix dough ingredients together.  Lightly dust a cutting board or silicone cutting mat with bean flour.  Roll out a tablespoon of dough at a time to about a 2 inch diameter.  Mix seasoning together. Lightly sprinkle seasoning on top of each pita and spread with fingers to evenly disburse spices. Do not over salt.  Slightly press seasoning into pita.  Cut each pita into 4 pie-shaped wedges.  Place wedges onto a baking sheet and bake at 350º for 10 minutes.  Makes 40 crisps.

## Basil Pita Crisps

½ cup oat bran
½ cup garbanzo bean flour
1½ tsp. baking powder
¼ tsp. salt
1 tsp. onion powder
1 tsp. dried basil
3 Tbsp. olive oil
1 egg

### Basil Seasoning:
1 Tbsp. dried basil
1 tsp. salt
1 tsp. garlic powder
1 tsp. onion powder
1 tsp. oregano
½ tsp. black pepper
¼ tsp. celery salt

Mix dough ingredients together.  Lightly dust a cutting board or silicone cutting mat with bean flour.  Roll out a tablespoon of dough at a time to about a 2 inch diameter.  Mix seasoning together. Lightly sprinkle seasoning on top of each pita and spread with fingers to evenly disburse spices. Do not over salt.  Slightly press seasoning into pita.  Cut each pita into 4 pie-shaped wedges.  Place wedges onto a baking sheet and bake at 350º for 10 minutes.  Makes 40 crisps.

**179**

## Gnocchi (Little Dumplings) (pasta substitute)

⅓-½ cup garbanzo bean flour
¼ cup oat bran, ground in a blender to a coarse flour
1 cup grated Parmesan cheese
2 eggs, slightly beaten
½ cup ricotta cheese, drained
½ tsp. onion powder

Place a pot of water on to boil. Combine ingredients in a bowl, starting with ⅓ cup garbanzo flour. Dough will be soft and sticky. Add remaining flour if dough is too soft. Using a teaspoon, scoop out about ½ tsp. dough for each gnoccho. Continue to scoop out spoons of dough and place onto waxed paper. Dip palms into water and roll dough into small balls about ½ inch in diameter. If desired, flatten dumplings with a fork. Press thumb into one side of gnocci, while pressing fork onto other side. When dumplings are formed, put small batches into gently boiling water. As soon as all the gnocchi float to the top, start timing. Let boil, uncovered, for 10 minutes. Remove from water with a slotted spoon and transfer to a serving bowl. Repeat with remaining batches. Serve with butter, salt, and pepper, or use in recipes to replace dumplings or noodles. These can be frozen in a single layer then transferred to freezer bag and stored in freezer. Thaw to use. Classic toppings include tomato sauces, pesto, or melted butter and Parmesan cheese. Makes about 3 cups.

## Pie Crust

1½ cups bean flour
1½ cups oat bran
½ tsp. salt
2 Tbsp. white vinegar
⅓ cup oil
⅓-½ cup water

Combine all ingredients, except water. Add water a little at a time to make a thick dough. Dough will be somewhat sticky. Divide dough in two. Press into an oil-sprayed pie plate or plates. To bake empty crust, bake at 400° for 10 minutes. Fill with any thick stew or casserole. To make top crust, roll ½ of dough between two pieces of plastic wrap. Wet counter to prevent wrap from slipping while rolling. Remove top wrap and turn crust onto filled pie. Remove second sheet of plastic. Seal edges or just trim edges and let dough float on top. Bake until top crust is browned. If bottom crust is baked and filling is hot, top crust should brown in 10-15 minutes at 400°. Use crust to create beef pot pie, chicken pot pie, etc. Makes two single pie crusts or one double crust.

## Carrot Muffins

1 cup safflower or walnut oil
3 eggs
1½ cups sifted garbanzo bean flour
½ cup oat bran
1 tsp. baking soda
1 tsp. allspice
½ tsp. nutmeg
½ tsp. salt
1½ tsp. vanilla
3½ cups coarsely chopped
   or grated carrots
1 cup coarsely chopped walnuts or pecans

Grease and flour muffin tins or use cupcake papers. Spray inside of papers with oil. Mix oil and eggs in a large bowl with a mixer. Beat in remaining ingredients, except carrots and nuts. Place carrots into a food processor and pulse until finely chopped. Stir carrots and nuts into muffin mixture. Fill muffin tins or papers ¾ full. Bake at 350° for 30-35 minutes, until a toothpick inserted in center comes out clean. Cool on a wire rack. Makes 24 muffins.

## Carrot Cake

1 recipe Carrot Muffin Batter
(above)

### Cream Cheese Icing:
16-oz. cream cheese
2½-3 cups whipped cream
1½ tsp. vanilla

Spray two 8" or 9" round cake pans with oil. Cut paper bag or waxed paper circles to fit in bottoms of pans. Mix together carrot muffin recipe and pour ½ of batter into each cake pan. Bake at 350° for 35 minutes, or until toothpick inserted in center comes out clean. Cool on wire racks. Place cream cheese in a mixing bowl. With a mixer, beat at high speed until fluffy. Add whipped cream and vanilla and beat at low speed until well blended. When cake has cooled, ice cake. Icing will be thin. Store in refrigerator.

Cake pictured was decorated by using carrot and avocado for coloring. For carrot coloring: grate half a carrot and boil in a small amount of water until carrot is soft. Place in cheesecloth bag and squeeze juice from carrots. If juice is too thin, place back in pot and boil until desired thickness (too thin and your icing will be runny). For avocado coloring, take a small piece of avocado and mash well. Mix the avocado with your icing for a light green tint.

**181**

## Pumpkin Muffins

½ cup oat bran
1 ½ cups garbanzo bean flour, sifted
1 tsp. salt
3 tsp. baking powder
1¼ tsp. ground nutmeg
1½ tsp. ground allspice
1/3 cup cold butter, cut into cubes
1 15-oz. can (2 cups) pumpkin
¾ cup evaporated milk

Whisk together flour, oat bran, salt, baking powder, nutmeg, and allspice. Place mixture into a food processor fitted with a metal blade. Add cold butter and pulse until mixture resembles coarse bread crumbs. Pour into a bowl and stir in pumpkin and milk. Mix well. Spoon mixture into oil-sprayed or paper-lined muffin tins. Bake at 450° for 8-10 minutes, until golden brown. Makes 12 muffins.

Variation: for **Pumpkin Peanut Butter Muffins**, add 1½ cups of peanut butter with the pumpkin and evaporated milk.

# Index

**187**

**190**